AF480178

INDIAN ART

Author: Robert Weinstein

Layout:
Baseline Co. Ltd,
District 3, Ho Chi Minh City
Vietnam

ISBN: 978-1-68325-926-8

Printed in

Robert Weinstein

INDIAN ART

Sacred traditions, temples, and timeless beauty

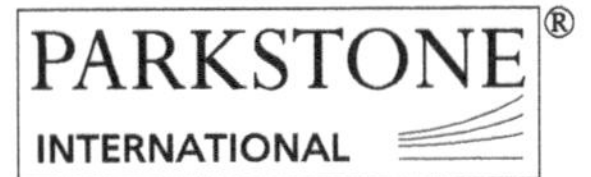

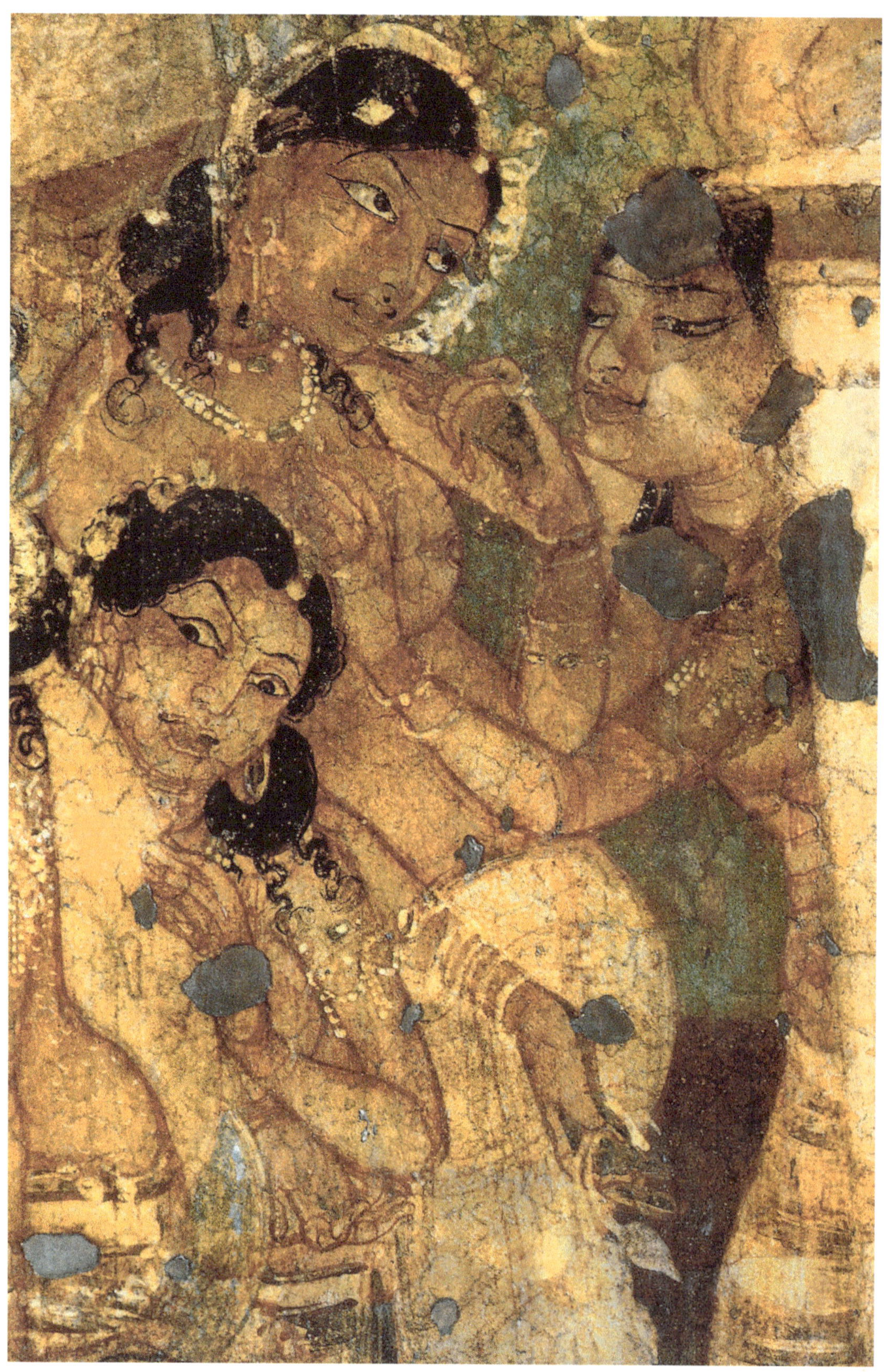

CONTENTS

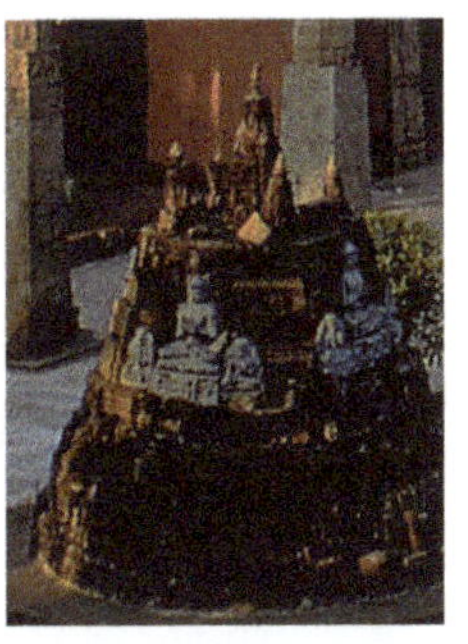
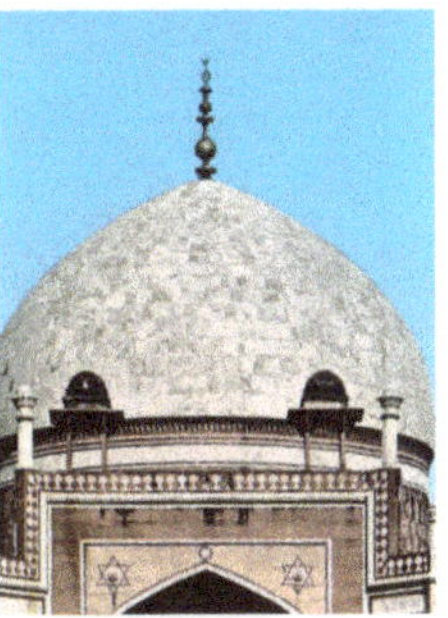
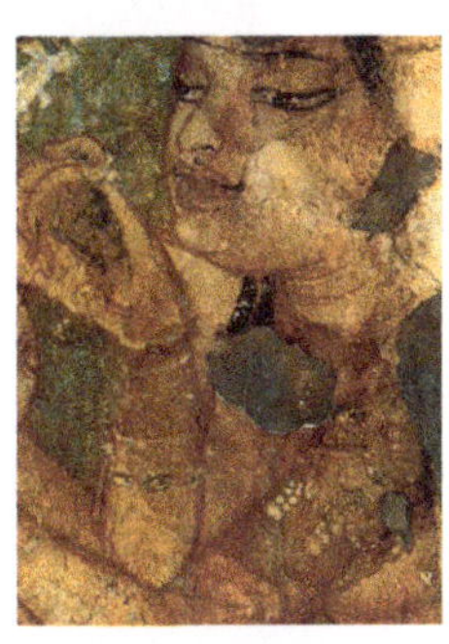
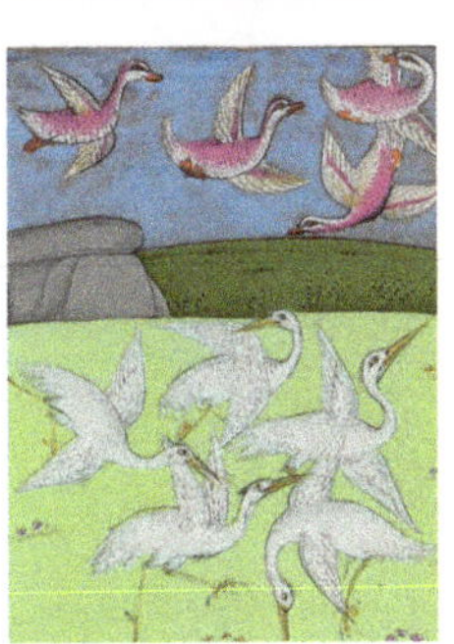
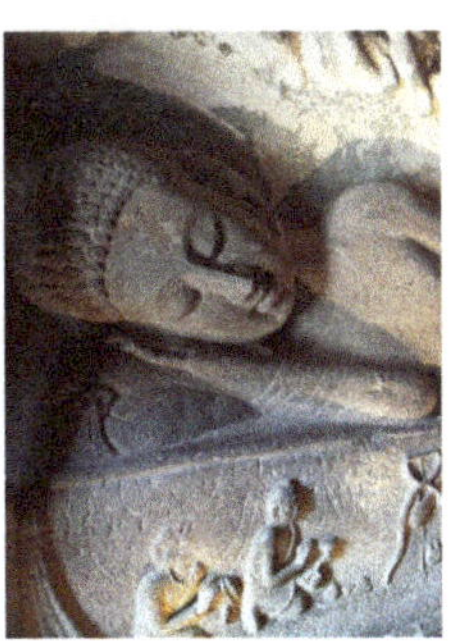

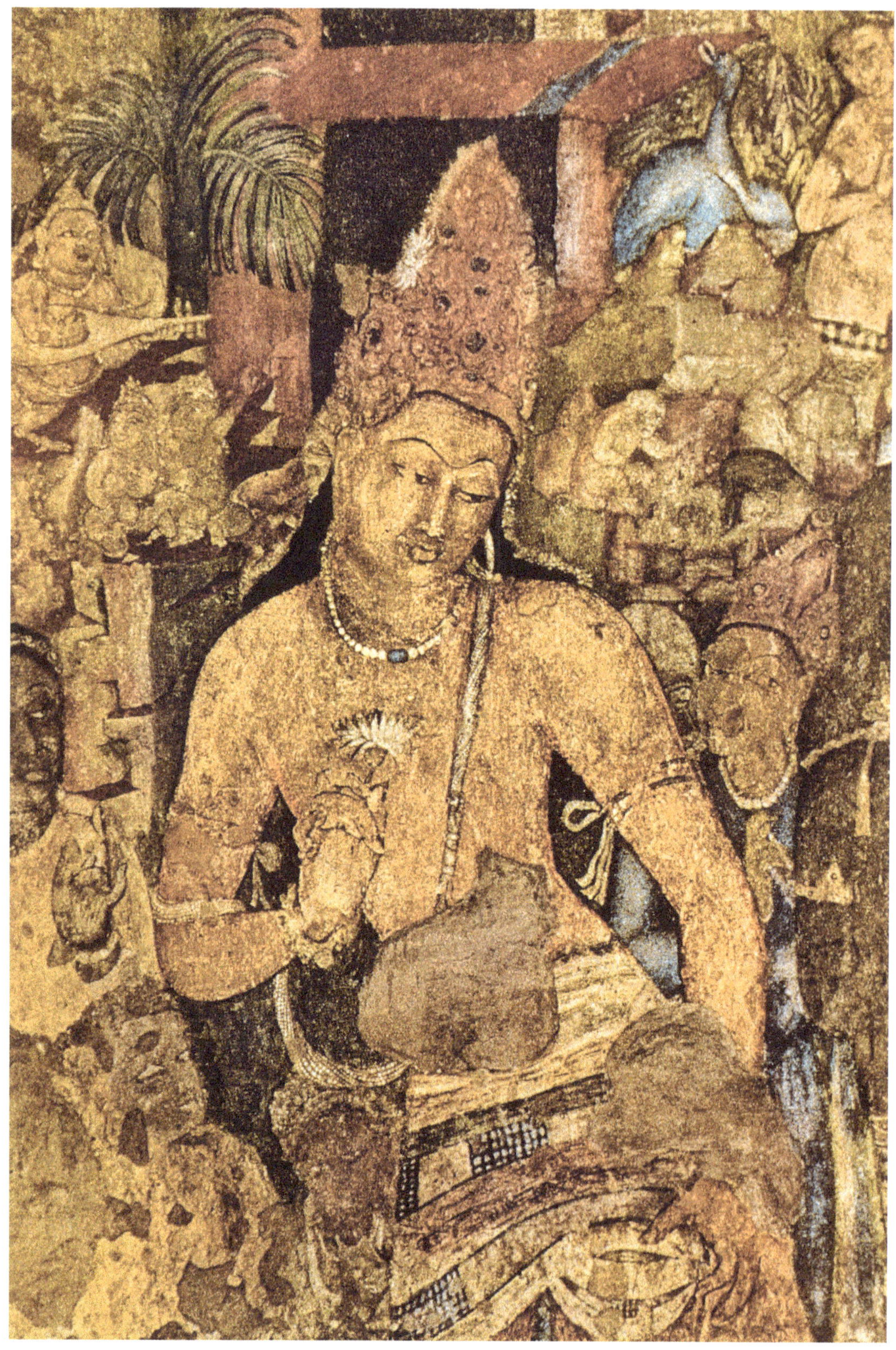

THE MAURYAN PERIOD

A short time after the death of Alexander in 323 B.C.E., the throne of Magadha, then the premier kingdom of Northern India, was seized by Chandragupta, surnamed the Maurya. In the course of a victorious reign of twenty-four years this able prince caused his influence to be felt over all India, at least as far south as the river Narmada.

Chandragupta was succeeded by his son Bindusara, who, in c. 273 B.C.E., transmitted the imperial scepter to his son, Ashoka, the third and most renowned sovereign of the Maurya dynasty. For forty-one years, Ashoka ruled his immense empire with great power and might, maintaining friendly relations with all his neighbors.

Early in life the emperor became a religious convert and as the years rolled by Ashoka's zeal increased. Finally, his energies and riches were almost entirely devoted to the patronage of the honoring and propagating the teaching of Gautama Buddhism. With one exception he abstained from wars of conquest and was thus free to concentrate his attention upon the task to which his life was consecrated.

Ashoka is credited by the literary sources with the use of masonry in the many building activities reported of him. He replaced the wooden walls and buildings of his capital by more substantial work and caused hundreds of fine edifices in both brick and stone to be erected throughout the empire. No building with any pretensions to be considered an example of architecture can be assigned to any earlier period than this, with which the history of Indian art and architecture begin. Whatever the true explanation of this may be the fact remains that the history of Indian art begins with Ashoka.

The pictorial character of the ancient Indian reliefs is obvious. The sudden adoption of stone as the material for both architecture and sculpture was in a large measure the result of foreign, perhaps Persian, example. Whatever the foreign elements of ancient Indian art may have been, great weight must be allowed for the personal

▲ *Maha-Janaka Jataka: Three of the queen's maids respond to the unexpected news that the king plans to renounce his worldly goods and leave their mistress*, late 6ᵗʰ century C.E., late Gupta period. Detail of a fresco. Ajanta caves (Cave I), near Aurangabad, Maharashtra.

◀ *The Bodhisattva Avalokitesvara (Bodhisattva of compassion)*, late 6ᵗʰ century C.E., late Gupta period. Detail of a fresco. Ajanta caves (cave I), near Aurangabad, Maharashtra.

initiative of Ashoka, a man of marked originality of mind, capable of forming large designs and executing them with imperial thoroughness.

Like most of the extant works of early Indian art, the Mauryan columns and caves were executed in honor of Buddhism, which became the state religion in the empire of Ashoka. Although we know that both Jainism and Brahmanical Hinduism continued to attract multitudes of adherents during the Mauryan period, hardly any material remains of works dedicated to the service of those religions have survived.

Isolated pillars, or columns, usually associated with other buildings, and frequently surmounted by a human figure, animal sculpture, or symbol have been erected in India at all times by adherents of all the three leading Indian religions. The oldest are the monolithic pillars of Ashoka, who set up at least thirty of these monuments, of which many survive. Ten of these bear his inscriptions. The Lauriya-Nandangarh monument, in Bihar, is the most graceful of all the Ashoka columns. The fabrication, conveyance, and erection of monoliths of such enormous size, the heaviest weighing about fifty tons, are proofs that the engineers and stonecutters of Ashoka's age were not inferior in skill and resource to those of any time or country.

The capital of each pillar, like the shaft, was monolithic, comprising three principal members, namely, a Persepolitan bell, abacus, and crowning sculpture in the round. The junction between the shaft and the abacus was marked by a necking, the edge of the abacus was decorated with bas-relief designs, and the crowning sculpture was occasionally a sacred symbol, such as a wheel, or more commonly a symbolic animal, or group of animals. The edge of the abacus of the beautiful Lauriya-Nandangarh pillar is decorated by a row of flying sacred geese in quite low relief. The topmost sculpture in the round was most often an elephant, a horse, a bull, or a lion.

The magnificent Sarnath capital discovered in 1905, unquestionably the best extant specimen of Ashokan sculpture, was executed late in the reign between 242 and 232 B.C.E. The column was erected to mark the spot where Gautama Buddha first publicly preached his doctrine. It would be difficult to find in any country an example of ancient animal sculpture superior to this beautiful work of art.

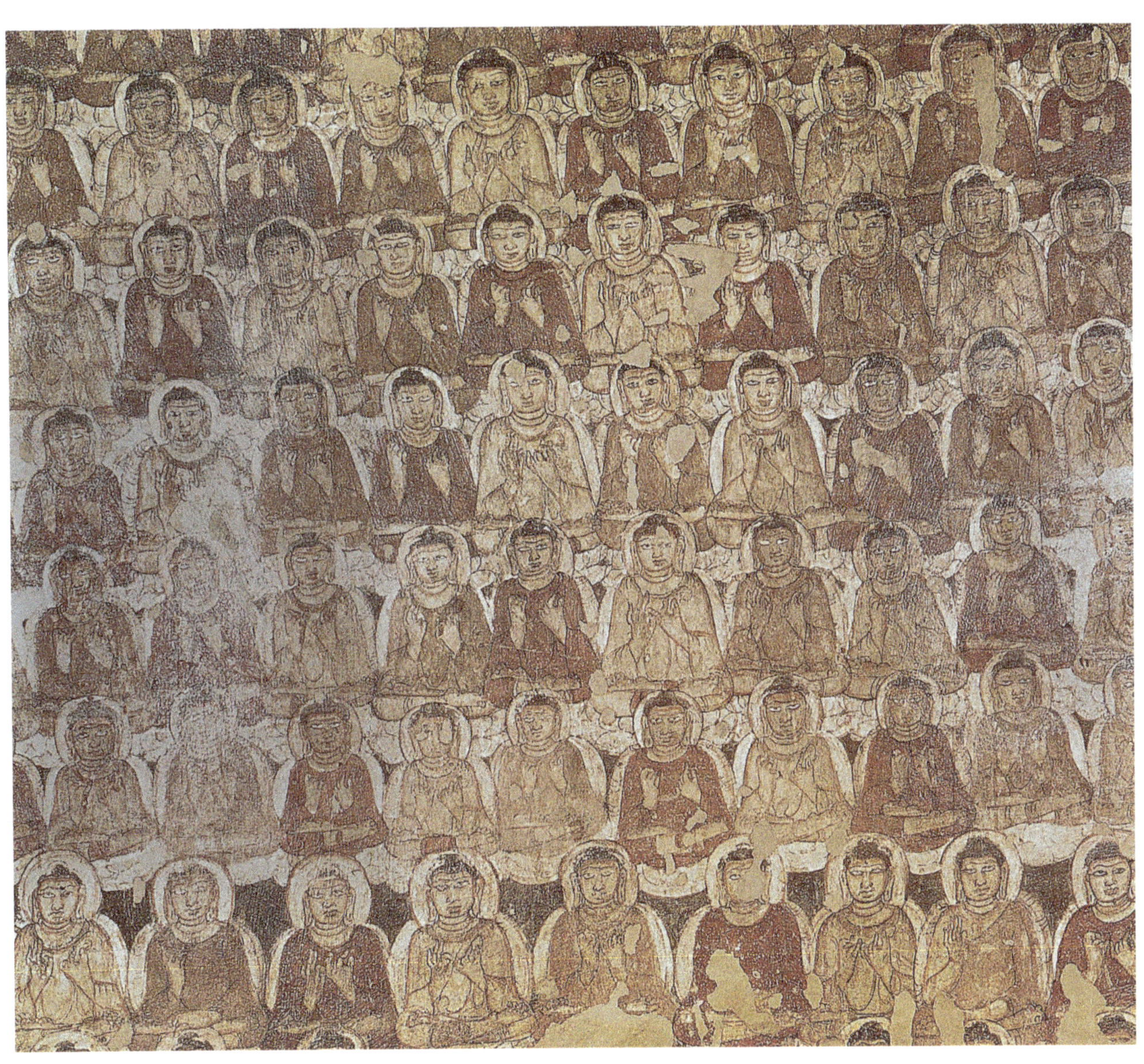

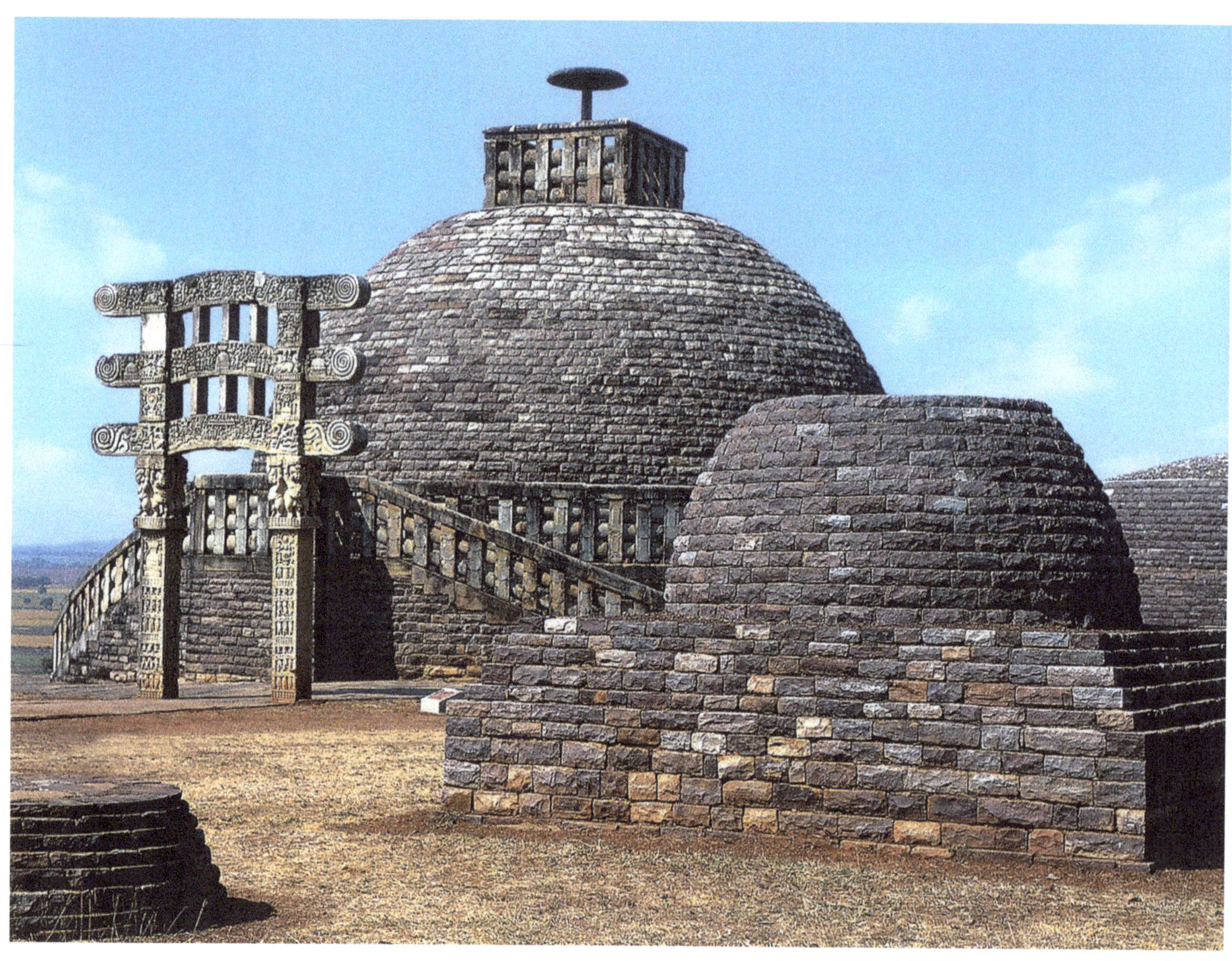

THE EARLY PERIOD

Architecture

After the death of Ashoka the empire broke to pieces, but his descendants continued to rule the home provinces for about half a century, at the end of which they were superseded by the Sunga kings who governed parts of Northern India. However, the style of architecture, decoration, and sculpture which perhaps first assumed a permanent form under the patronage of Ashoka continued in use up to about the close of the first century of the Common Era, forming a distinct and definite period in the history of Indian art.

Although Buddhism at this period, extending from 273 B.C.E. to 100 C.E., was by no means the only religion in India, it enjoyed a dominant position and the monuments remaining are almost all Buddhist, though few are as early as the reign of Ashoka.

The ancient civil buildings having all perished utterly, the story of Indian architecture must therefore be reconstructed from the somewhat one-sided evidence of the temples and shrines, and the bas-reliefs that adorn them. The most characteristic early architectural compositions were stupas, the most ancient of which were very plain. They were usually surrounded by a stone railing, sometimes square in plan, but more often circular, marking off a procession path for the use of worshippers and serving as a defense against evil spirits.

Bharhut and Sanchi represent two sequent stages in the development of the stupa of the Early Period. Sculpture was freely applied to every member of the railing to the posts, rails, and coping. Late in the second century of the Common Era at Amaravati the railing was transformed into a screen covered with stone pictures in comparatively low relief. The openings giving access to the procession path inside the railing were dignified by the creation of lofty gateways covered with a profusion of sculpture. The best examples of such gateways are those at Sanchi.

The origin of the stupa lies in primitive burial ceremonies for they are primarily tombs. Originally mounds of earth, the earliest stupas existing are of unbaked brick, hemispherical in shape. Although their first object was the enshrinement of sacred relics, in later times they acquired a symbolic value.

◀ *Stupa III of Sanchi*, 150-140 B.C.E., Sunga dynasty. Sandstone, stupa: diameter at the plinth: 15 m, height: 8.1 m. Sanchi, Madhya Pradesh.

Although monastic institutions in India were not confined to the Buddhists, the Buddhist Sangha (community) attained a height of power and a detail of organization to which the Jain and Brahmanical communities never aspired. In consequence, the buildings dedicated to the use of the Order were frequently designed on a scale of the utmost magnificence. The central and all important building of the early monasteries seems to have been the Sabha or hall of meeting of the community.

A great school of art is preserved for us in the great rock-cut halls and dwelling caves of Western India. Here, have been hewn out of the very heart of the rock full-scale reproductions of the ancient assembly halls in all the detail of their wooden construction. In general plan they correspond with the barrel-roofed buildings of the early sculpture. They are apsidal with side aisles on either hand and are lit by the great horseshoe window at one end. A survey of this series of caves lays bare a stylistic advance from purely wooden imitation to definitely lithic forms.

Sculpture

The art of the times is thoroughly human, a mirror of the social and religious life of ancient India, apparently a much pleasanter and merrier life than that of the India of later ages, when the Brahmans had reasserted their superiority and imposed their ideas upon art and upon every branch of Hindu civilization. The early sculptures, while full of the creatures of gay fancy, are free from the gloom and horror of the conceptions of the medieval artists.

The Buddhism was the popular creed of men and women living a natural life in the world, seeking happiness, and able to enjoy themselves.

The study of the existing monuments of Ashoka, scanty as they are, leaves one with a clear impression of a definite and distinct school of sculpture, with great stylistic and architectonic qualities and certain characteristics which distinguish it from the sculpture of the Early Period and from all other periods of Indian art. Firstly, finely stylized as these works are they are essentially naturalistic. Secondly, columns, capitals, and caves all have a highly finished, polished surface which is unique and unmistakable.

Among these sculptures, which are mostly of colossal size, is a mutilated standing statue of a male, perhaps representing the Yaksha demigod Kuvera, god of wealth. The material is polished grey sandstone similar to that used for the Ashoka pillars. The excessively massive body, which possesses considerable grandeur, is clothed in a waistcloth held around the loins by means of a flat girdle tied in a knot in front. The ornaments are a necklace and a torque from which four tassels hang down on the back. This is probably the earliest example of 'early' sculpture as distinct from the Mauryan. In treatment and detail it is clearly a forerunner of the sculpture of Bharhut

▶ *The Great Stupa of Sanchi*, 3rd century B.C.E., Sunga dynasty. Sandstone, stupa: diameter at the plinth: 37 m, height: 16.5 m, stone railing: 30.8 m. Sanchi, Madhya Pradesh.

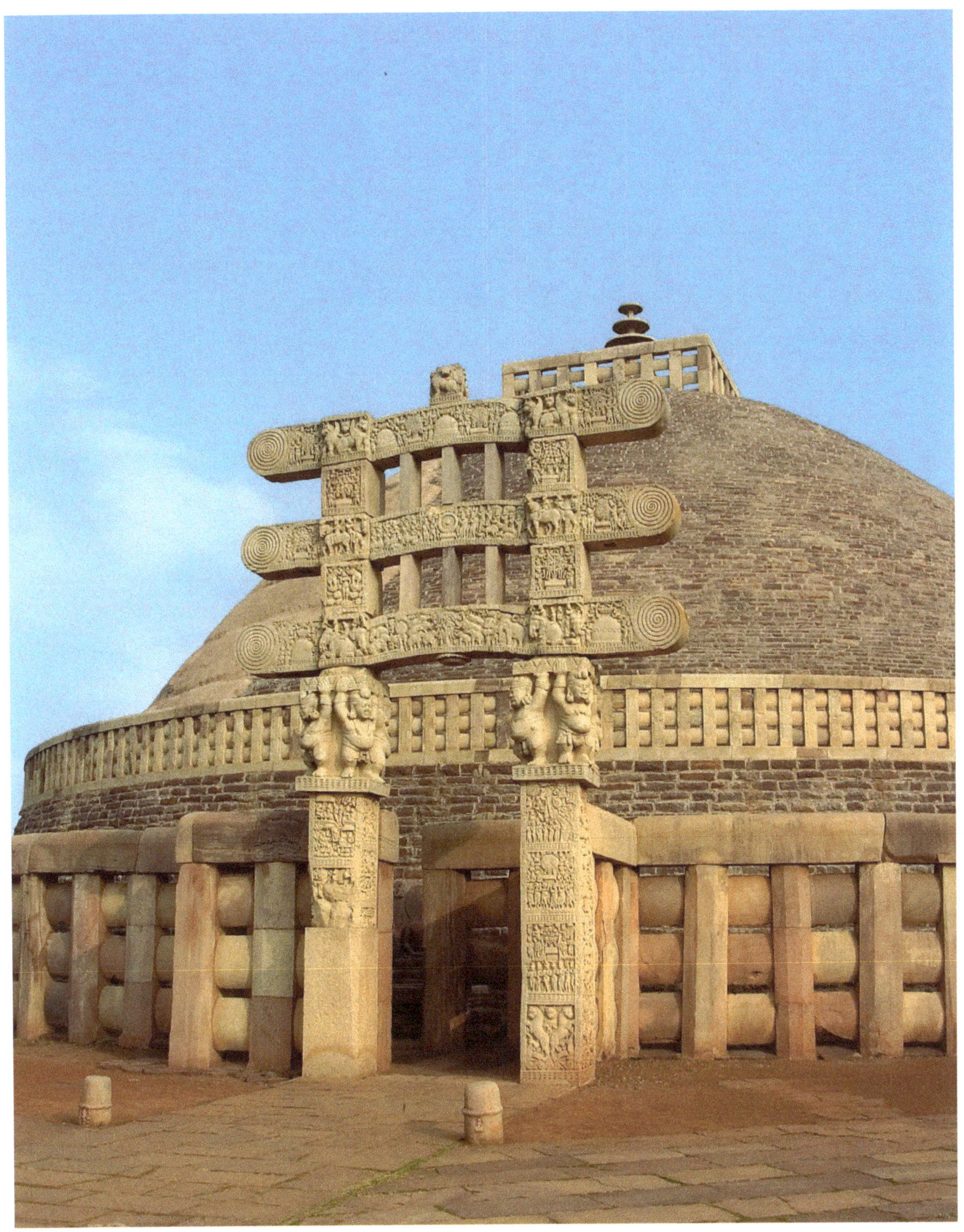

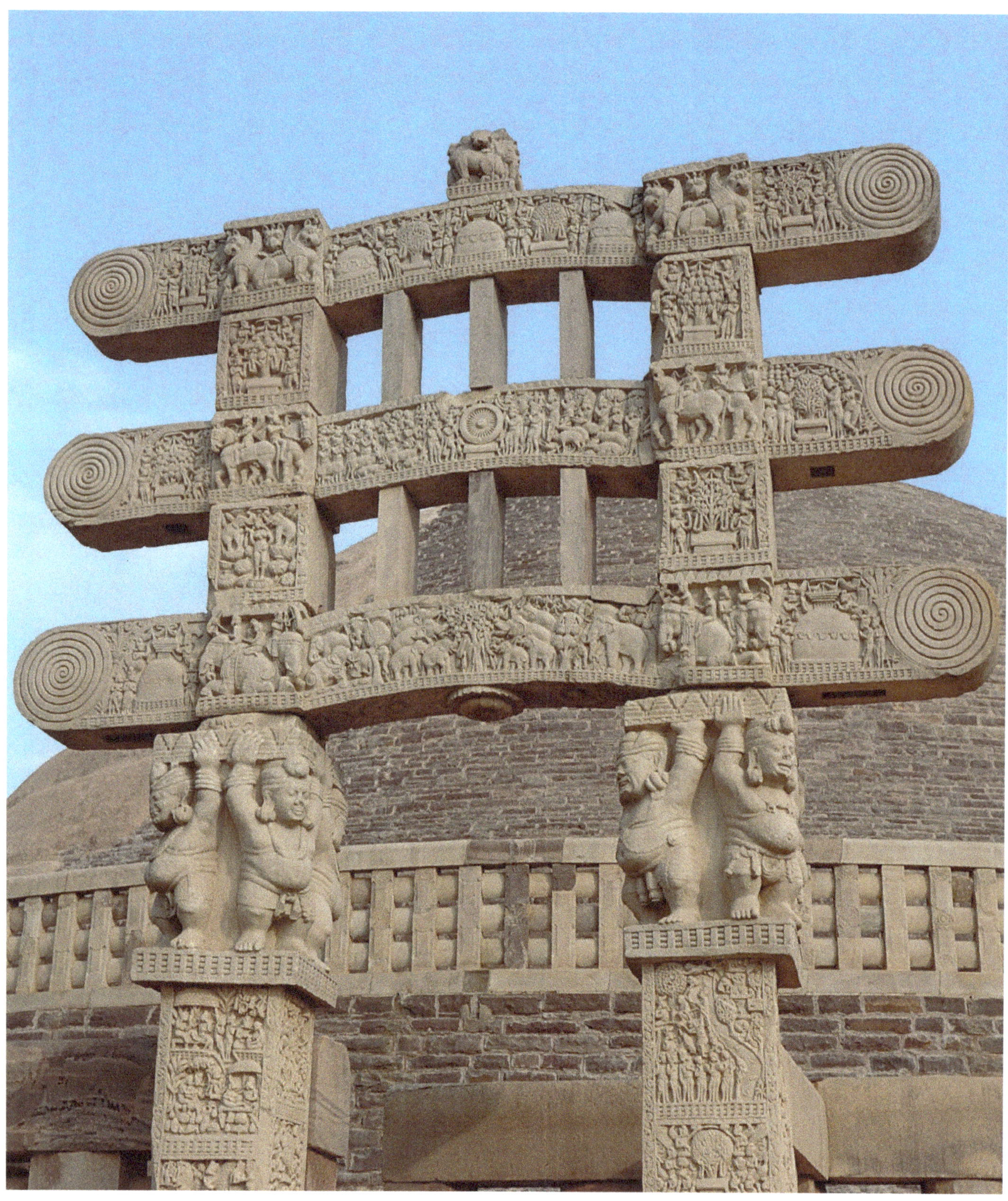

and has nothing in common with the art of the Mauryan capitals. Several other colossal sculptures emphasize this development.

The medallions on the rail bars and the half-medallions on the pillars are filled with a wonderful variety of bas-relief subjects. The comic monkey scenes display a lively sense of humor, freedom of fancy and clever drawing. The rollicking humor and liberty of fancy unchecked by rigid canons, while alien to the transcendental philosophy and ascetic ideals of the Brahmans, are thoroughly in accordance with the spirit of Buddhism. Everything seems to indicate that India was a much happier land in the days when Buddhism flourished than it has ever been since.

The Bharhut sculptures, having escaped the destructive zeal of Islamic iconoclasts by reason of their situation in an out-of-the-way region, lay safely hidden under a thick veil of jungle until, when the establishment of general peace and the spread of cultivation stimulated the local rustics to construct substantial houses from the spoils of the old monuments. The extensive group of early Buddhist buildings at and near Sanchi in the Bhopal State similarly evaded demolition because it lay out of the path of the armies of Islam. However, the monuments of Sanchi have

not wholly escaped injury from the ravages of the village builders and during the first half of the nineteenth century much damage was done by the ill-advised curiosity of amateur archaeologists. Nowadays, however, everything possible is being done to conserve the local memorials of India's ancient greatness.

The importance of Sanchi in the history of Indian art rests chiefly upon the four wonderful gateways forming the entrances to the procession path between the stupa and the surrounding railing. A key to the chronology of the site is provided by the Ashoka column which stands to the right of the South gateway. The Mauryan level is marked by a floor of pounded earth and clay. Three other levels or floors appear over it, the topmost being lime-plastered. Sanchi has taken on a new lease of life and beauty, the most important remains of this huge site being carefully restored and preserved.

All the Sanchi sculptures, like the Ajanta paintings, deal with Buddhist subjects if a composition seems in our eyes to be purely secular, that is only because we do not understand its meaning. The main object of the artist was to illustrate his Bible. In addition to his desire to tell edifying stories in a manner readily intelligible to the eyes of the faithful, the artist clearly was dominated by the feeling that he was bound to impress on all beholders the lesson that the dead Teacher, the last and greatest of the long line of Buddhas, had won and continually received the willing homage of the whole creation. And so, in all the ancient Buddhist art, whether at Sanchi or elsewhere, weird winged figures hovering in the air, snake-headed or fishtailed monsters emerging from their caverns or haunting the deep, offer their silent homage to the Lord of all, and the monkeys bow down in adoration before the Master who had turned the wheel of the Law and set it rolling through the world.

The early artists did not dare to portray his bodily form, being content to attest his spiritual presence by silent symbols, the footprints, the empty chair, and so forth. But, whether the Master was imaged or symbolized, the notion of his adoration by all creation was continually present in the minds of the artists. Although concerned in the main with thoughts of religion they were not unmindful of beauty, which they often succeeded in attaining in no small degree.

Surveying the work of the Early Period (second century B.C.E.-early first century C.E.) one recognizes certain distinctive common elements: the absence of the Buddha figure; its replacement by certain simple symbols; and the popular quality of the work, the living oral tradition of which is indicated by the predominance of Jataka scenes even over the scriptural; the naive technique which treats each story as a pictorial entity contained in a single panel or medallion.

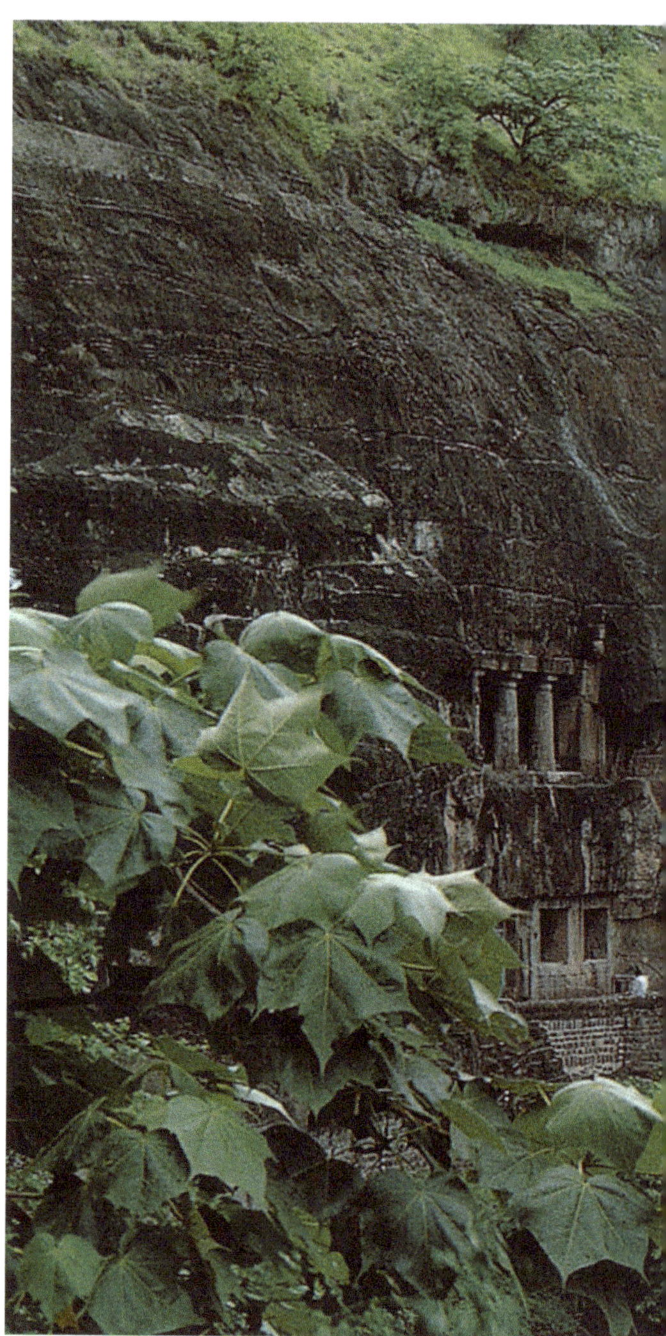

▶ *Ajanta caves*, 5th-6th century C.E., late Gupta period. Rock-cut. Ajanta caves (Caves XXIII-XXVII), near Aurangabad, Maharashtra.

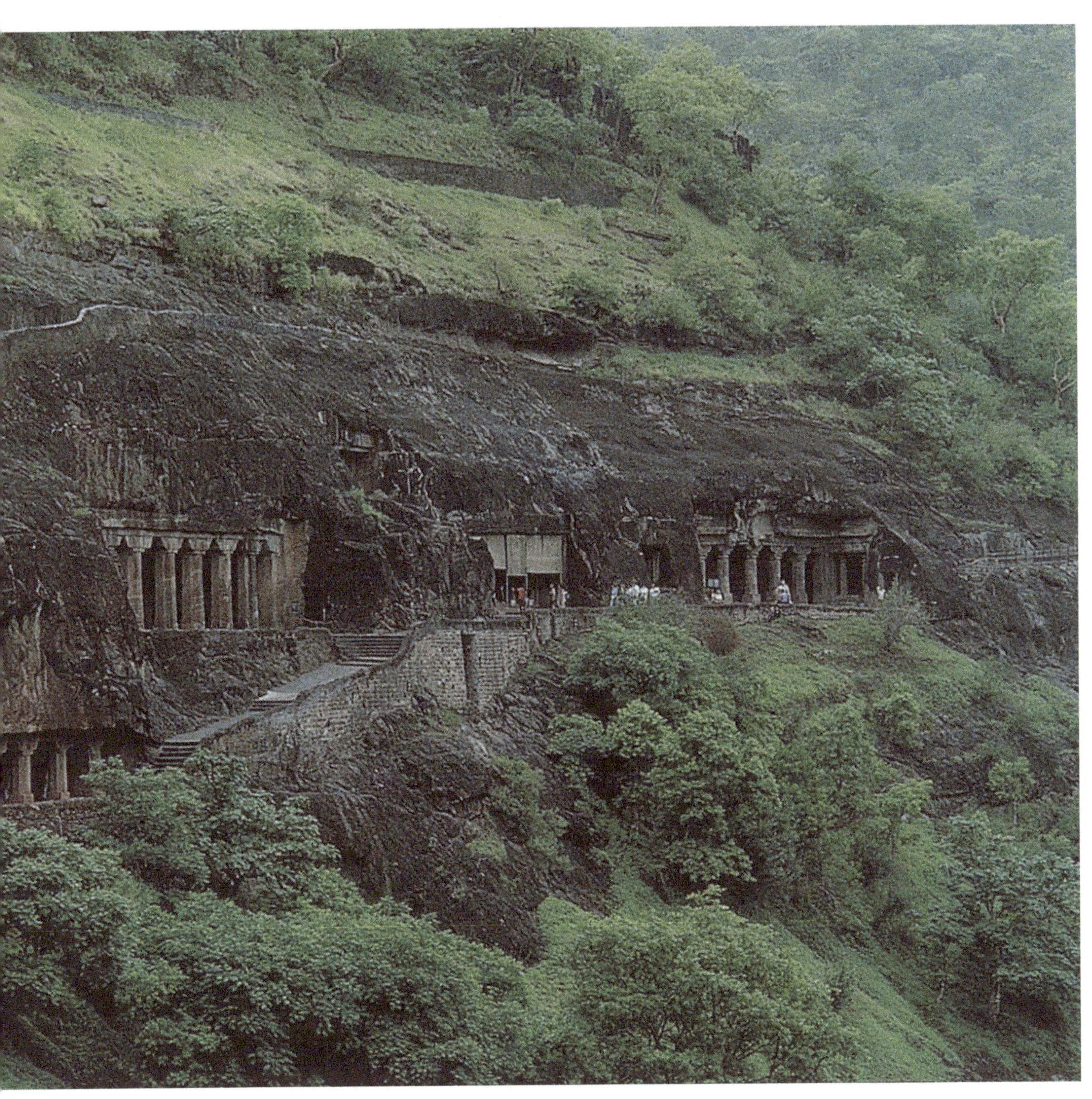

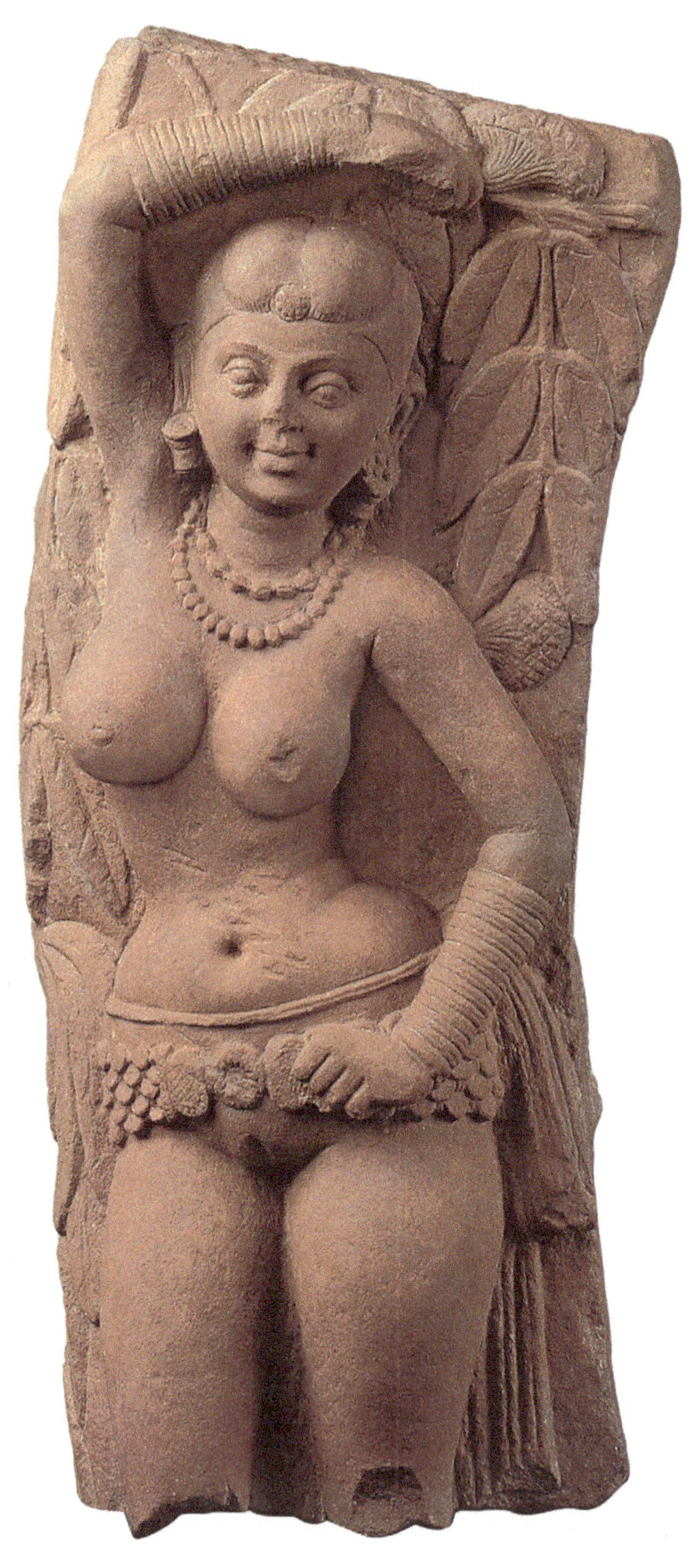

THE KUSHAN, LATER ATAVAHNA, AND IKSHVAKU PERIODS

Mathura

Mathura is the chief find spot of Kushan sculpture. Six sovereigns of the dynasty are of importance for the history of India and of Indian art. The first two are most conveniently cited as Kadphises I (reign 45 to 50 C.E.) and II (reign 50 to 85 C.E.). The next four kings, Kanishka, Vasishka, Huvishka, and Vasudeva I, reigned in that order for a century.

In the early centuries of the Common Era Mathura on the Jumna, a city of immemorial antiquity, and prosperous to this day was sacred in the eyes of the adherents of all the three indigenous Indian religions Jainism, Buddhism, and Brahmanical Hinduism. The abundant supply of excellent red sandstone at Rupbas and other quarries favored the development of an active school of sculptors, whose workshops supplied all parts of Northern India with idols. The character of the local stone is so distinct that the products of the Mathura studios are easily recognized wherever they may be found.

Sarnath, like Mathura, was holy ground to the Jains as well as the Buddhists, and is connected with Mathura and declared a Kushan site of importance by finds of fine sculptures of red Mathura sandstone inscribed in the Kushan era. Its richly adorned buildings, crowded with sculpture, were involved in common ruin by the violence of the fierce hosts of Islam at the close of the twelfth century.

The Mathura sculptures are definitely comparable to Bharhut and Sanchi, but it is evident that the tradition was never broken, Kushan sculpture springing directly from the older school. Most of these sculptures had as their function the adornment of Jain or Buddhist stupas and consist chiefly of railing pillars and medallions. Many of the ancient motives are preserved such as the bull and the fish-elephant (*makara*). The bracket figure is a development of the woman-and-tree motif used for the same structural purpose as at Sanchi. The work of this period shows an increasing schematic and patterned quality, well illustrated in the knotted foliage. The excavations at Mathura have yielded

◀ A gateway bracket decorated with a yakshi holding a branch (repeated on the opposite side). The figure wears courtly jewellery, including an elaborate belt and sash that secure a diaphanous skirt. This bracket belonged to a ceremonial gateway (torona) marking an entrance to a shrine, most probably a Buddhist stupa, 2nd *century, Kushan period, Mathura, Uttar Pradesh. Mottled red sandstone, 51 x 22 x 23 cm. Purchased from Imre Schwaiger in 1927, Victoria & Albert Museum, London.*

numerous specimens of pillars of stone railings associated with stupas, both Jain and Buddhist. The pillars have high-relief statuettes, usually of females, on the front, and other paneled scenes one above the other, or floral patterns on the back.

A certain group of sculptures from Mathura or its neighborhood, all dealing with strong drink and intoxication, which may be classed together as 'Bacchanalian', have excited much interest and discussion. The supposed Greek character of these sculptures, when first discovered, was much exaggerated by the early commentators. The front group comprises four persons in two pairs, each consisting of a man and woman standing under an Ashoka tree in flower. The stout man on the right has his left arm round the waist of his female companion, who holds his right hand in hers, thus giving him the support rendered necessary by his intoxicated condition, due to the liquor, pots of which stand on the ground.

The reeling man wears nothing except a pair of short swim shorts, and a scarf hanging behind his back and fastened round his neck by a knot. The slighter and perfectly sober man on the left is decently dressed in long drawers extending to his ankles. Both of the women are clad in a short tunic coming down a little below the waist. Each holds a piece of loose drapery. The woman on the left has it thrown over her left arm in the fashion adopted by some of the Gandhara Bodhisattvas. Both women are adorned with heavy Indian anklets, armlets, and collars.

The reverse group, much mutilated, comprises five figures, of whom the principal is a fat elderly man

sitting on a stone seat with his left leg tucked up, and so drunk that he has to be supported on his left side by a man and a boy and on his right by a woman. The drunkard wears a waistcloth, loosely fastened. In style both reliefs are similar. The front group, however, differs from its companion. Five figures under an Ashoka tree again appear. The principal is a fat man, seemingly nude, seated with his left leg tucked up, on a low heap of stones laid in courses.

Besides the Kushan Buddhas or Bodhisattvas and the Nagas, various Kushan canonical scenes are found in bas-reliefs. A common representation is the visit of Indra to Buddha in the Indrasila cave. The mountainous locality is conventionally indicated by 'rockwork' and its desolateness by birds and beasts looking out from their lairs. A tablet with relief sculpture represents a three-tiered Jain stupa with trees on either side of it and pairs of harpies and centaurs bringing offerings and garlands. These 'offering-bearer' scenes are very common.

Amaravati

The stupa of Amaravati in its earliest form was of high antiquity, dating, as inscriptions prove, from about 200 B.C.E. But the great mass of the sculpture is much later, and belongs to the

▶ *Lady with mirror*, 2nd century, Kushan period. Spotted red sandstone, height: 108 cm. Mathura, Uttar Pradesh.

▶ *Woman with pot and grapes*, 2nd century, Kushan period. Red sandstone, height: 132 cm. Mathura, Uttar Pradesh.

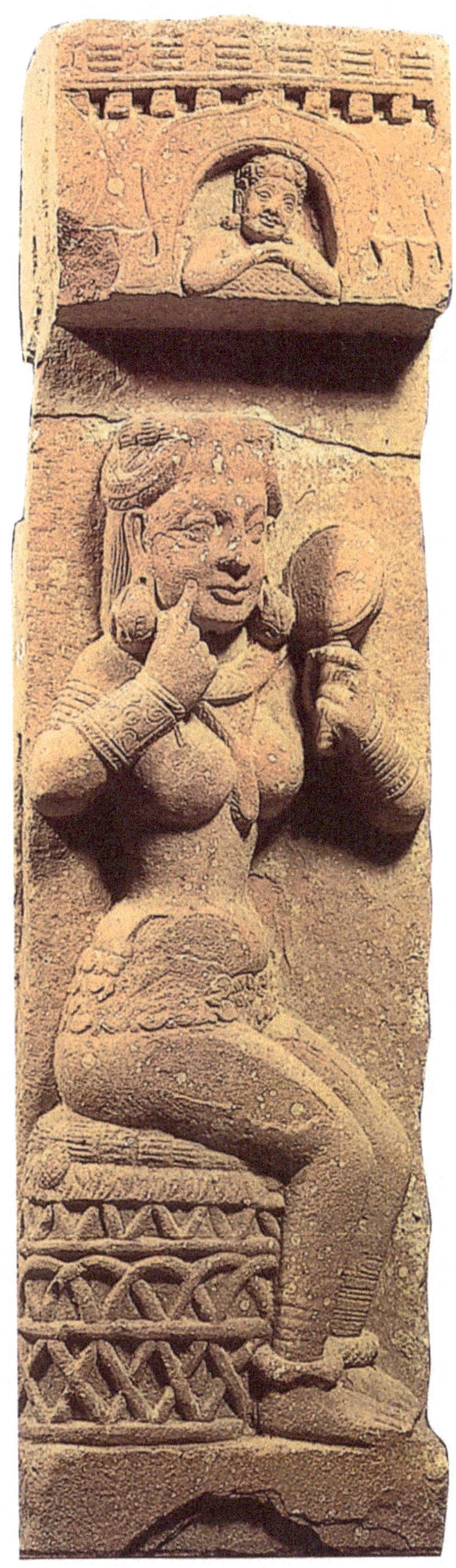
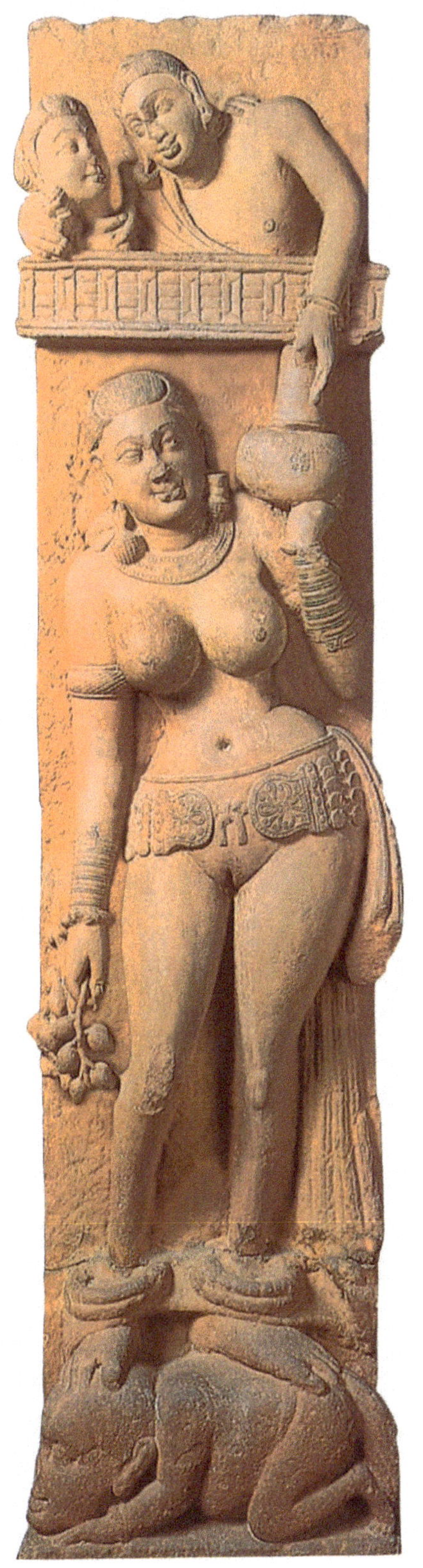

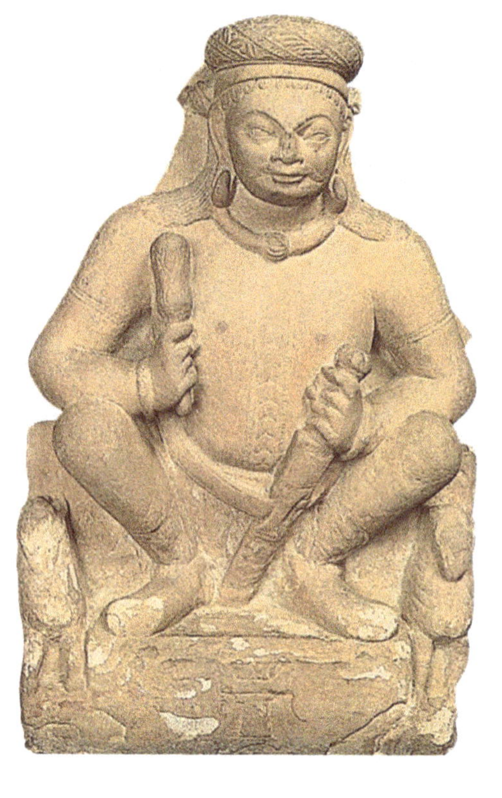
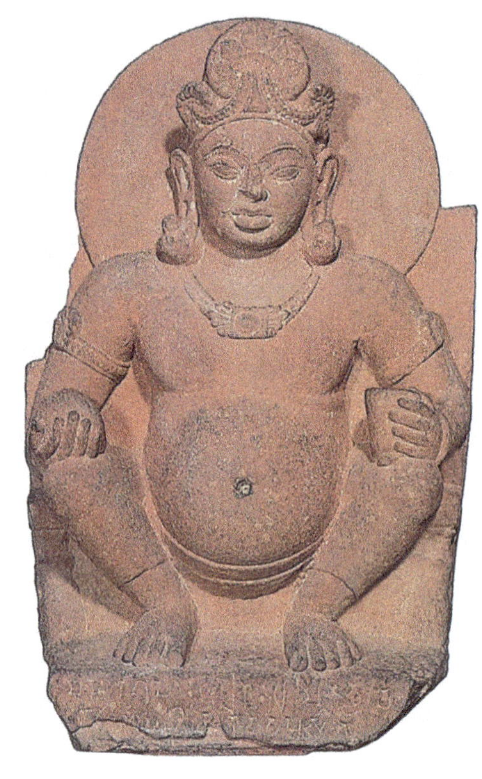
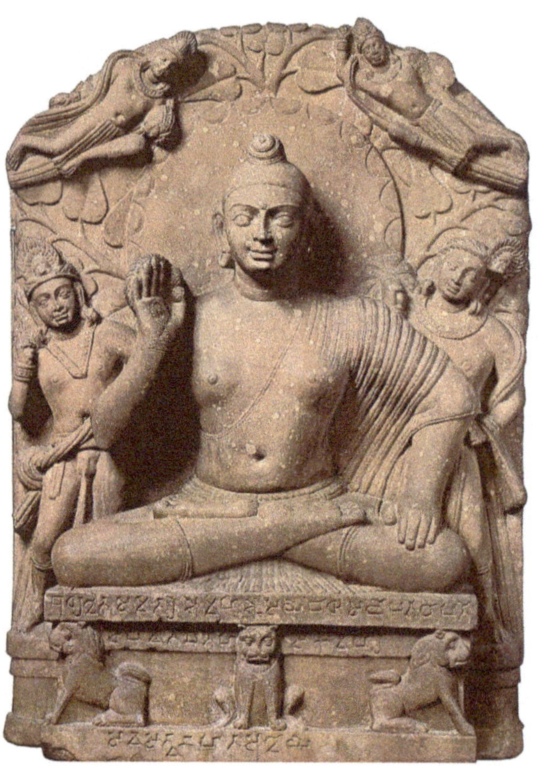
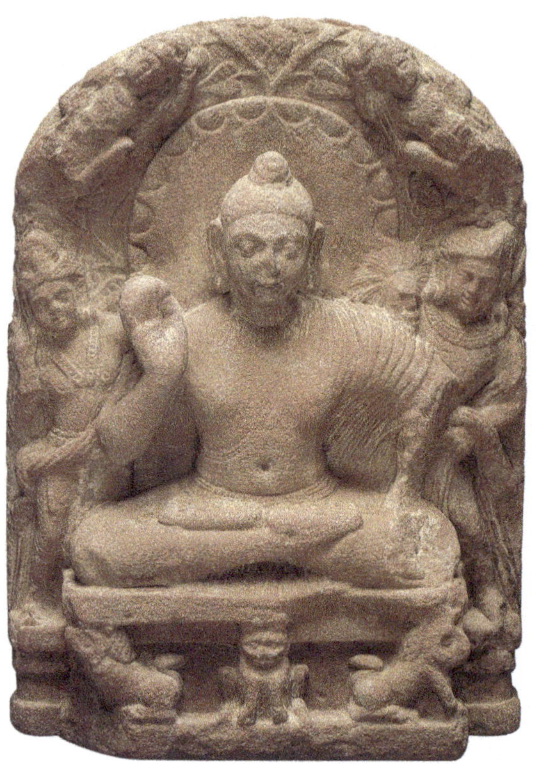

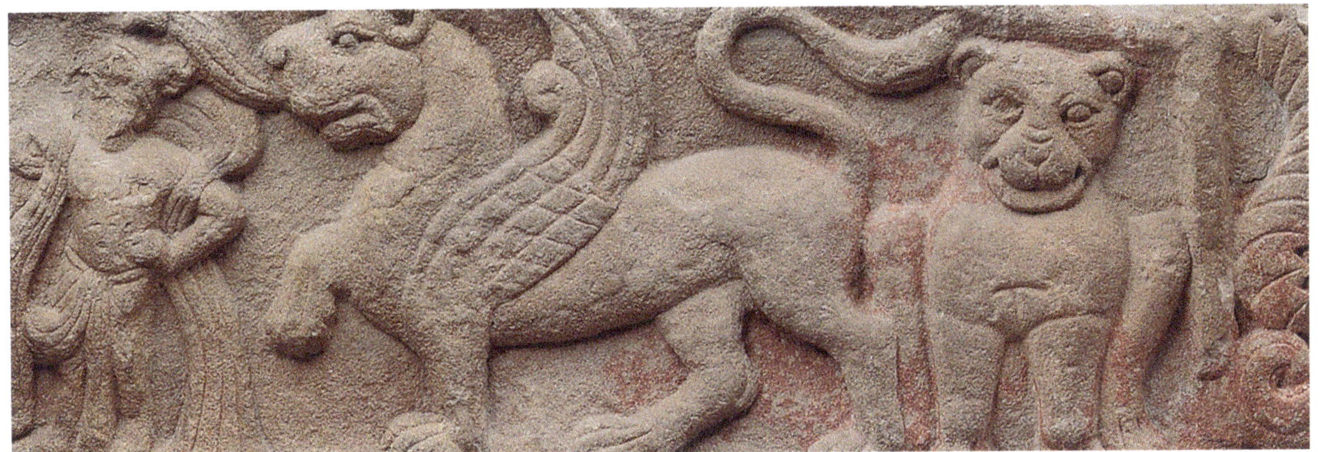

Kushan period. The small town of Amaravati on the south bank of the Krishna river represents a more important ancient city called Dharanikota. A richly decorated stupa, known to have been in good repair and still venerated in the twelfth century, continued to exist up to the close of the eighteenth or the beginning of the nineteenth century, when it was utterly destroyed by a greedy local landholder, eager to obtain cheap building material. Various archaeological explorers have salved remnants of the sculptures, which are now mostly housed in the British Museum or the Central Museum, Madras.

It may be true that originally the effect of the Amaravati marbles was heightened by color. But whether they were painted or not, they must have formed, when perfect, one of the most splendid exhibitions of artistic skill known in the history of the world.

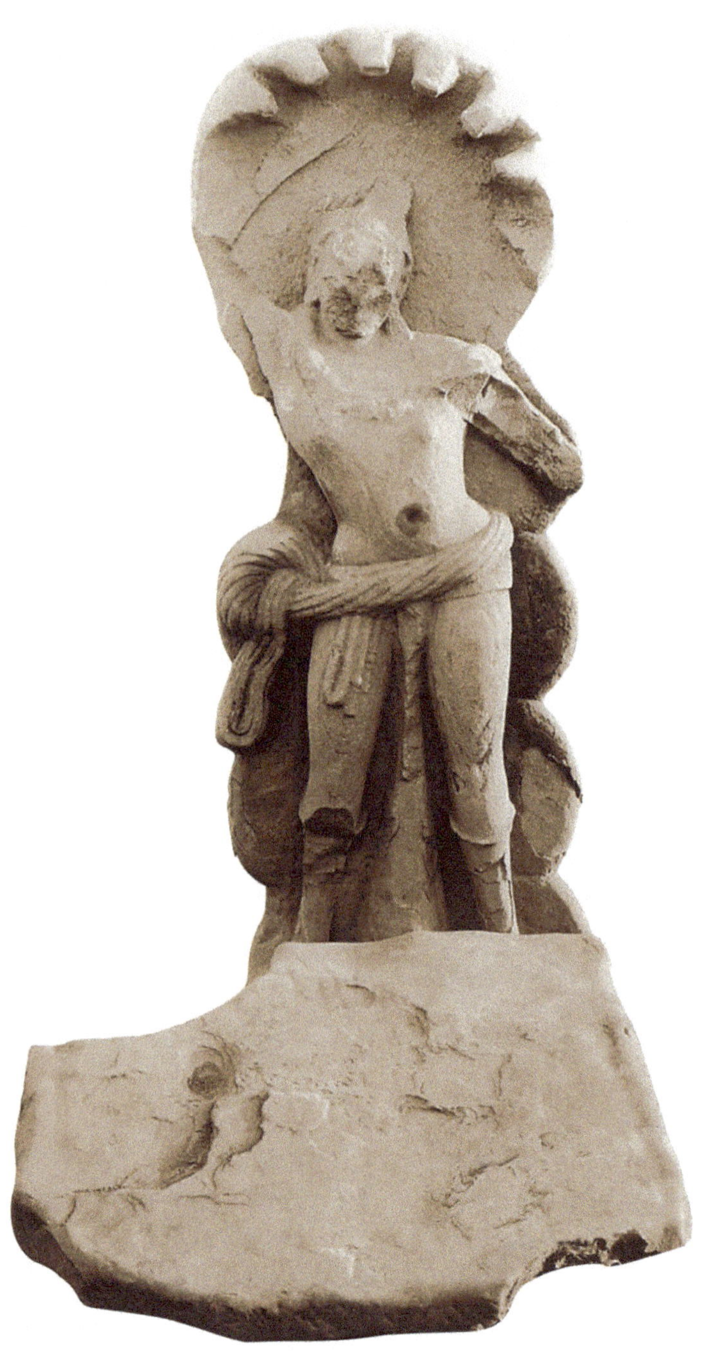

▲ *Nagaraja, a snake-king, lord of the underworld*, 167 C.E.,
Kushan period, Chhargaon, Uttar Pradesh.
Sandstone, height: 152.4 cm.
Mathura Museum, Uttar Pradesh.

▶ *Buddha Sakyamuni standing*, first half of 2nd century B.C.E.,
Kushan period. Red sandstone, height: 172 cm.
Private collection, Mathura, Uttar Pradesh.

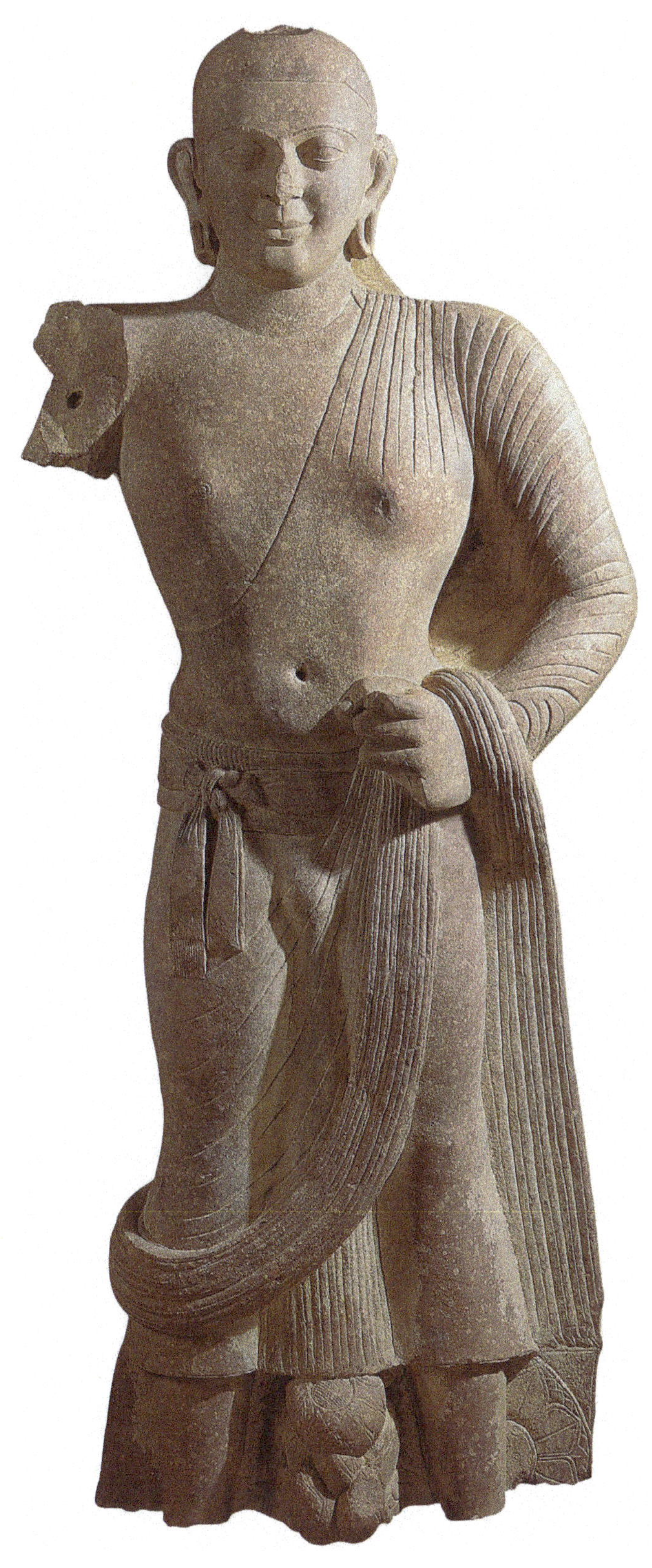

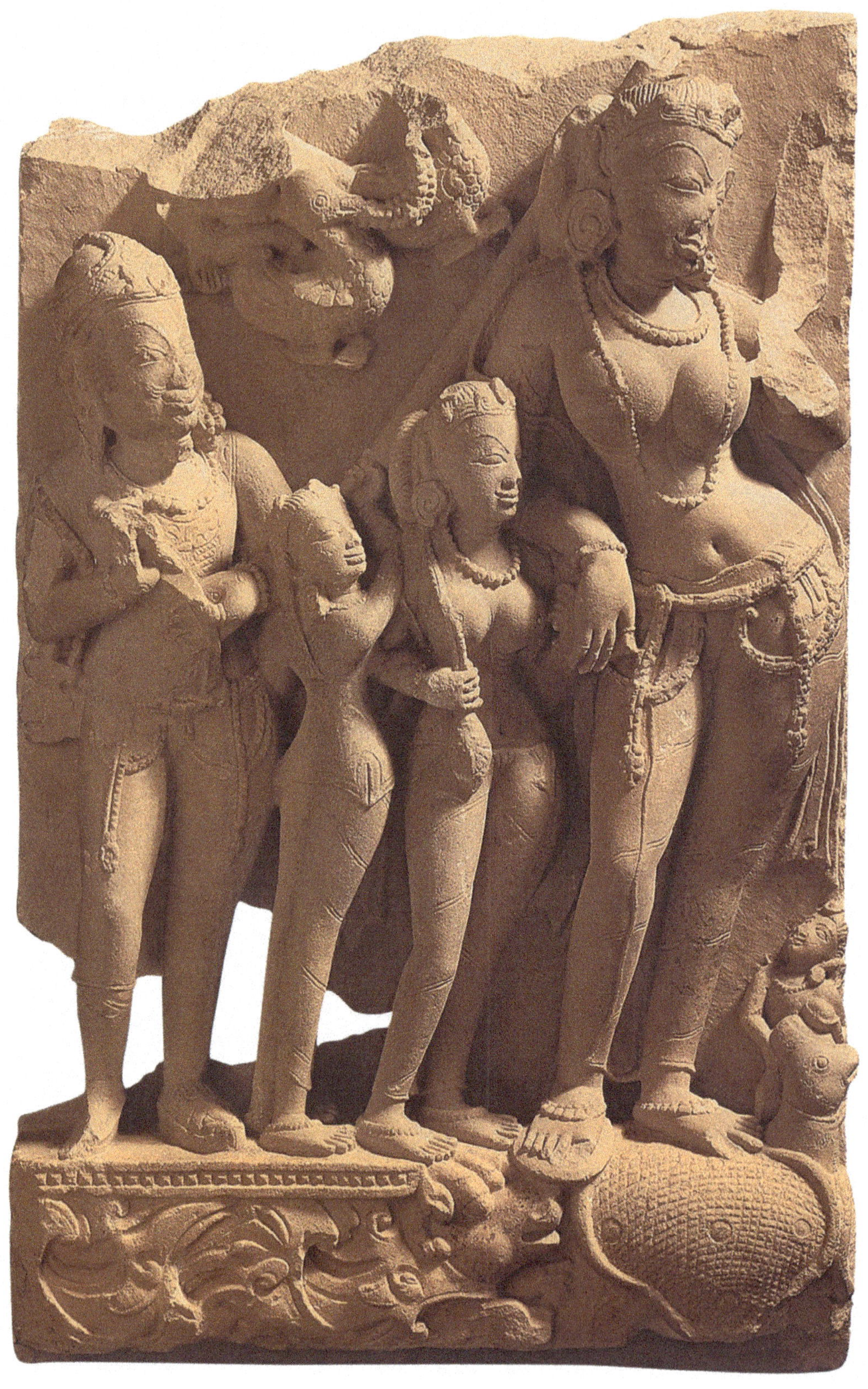

THE GUPTA PERIOD

The displacement of the Arsacid by the Sassanian dynasty of Persia III 226 C.E., the approximately simultaneous downfall of the Andhra kings who had ruled the Deccan for four and a half centuries, and the disappearance of the Kushan or Indo-Scythian sovereigns of Northern India about the same time, unquestionably must have resulted in violent political and social disturbances on Indian soil during the third century. But hardly any record, archaeological or literary, has survived of that stormy interlude.

The rise of the Imperial Gupta dynasty in 320 C.E., with its capital at Pataliputra (Patna), marks the beginning of a new epoch. Under a succession of able and long-lived monarchs the Gupta dominions rapidly increased, until in the first quarter of the fifth century they comprised much of the Indian subcontinent.

During the last quarter of the fifth century the Gupta empire was shattered by the inrush of swarms of fierce Huns and allied nomad tribes from Central Asia. The short-lived Hun power was broken in India by a decisive victory gained by native princes about 528 C.E., but a long time elapsed before new political combinations of any stability could be formed. In the seventh century a great king named Harsha (590-647 C.E.) conquered India north of the Narmada, while the Deccan submitted to his able contemporary Pulakesin II (Chalukya), and the far south was governed by a powerful Pallava king. The Chalukya fell before the Pallava in 642, and five or six years later, Harsha died childless, leaving the empire which he had won a prey to anarchy.

During the seventh and eighth centuries the foreign settlers had become Hinduised, tribes developing into castes. When the ninth century opens we find a new distribution of power among kingdoms mostly governed by so-called Rajputs. The Hun invasions with the subsequent readjustments mark the division between the history of Ancient and that of Medieval India.

During the reigns of Chandragupta II and his next two successors, from about 375 to 490 C.E., every branch of Hindu literature, science, and art was vigorously cultivated under the stimulus of liberal royal patronage; and the greatest of Indian poets graced the Gupta court and produced his

◄ *Yamuna, the personification of the river Yamanu (Jamna), is represented riding on a tortoise (kuma) and is attended by two handmaidens - one supporting her umbrella. Together with Ganga, these two river goddesses flank a temple doorway, cleansing those who enter from the material world to the palace of the gods*, c. 900 C.E., Gurjara-Pratihara dynasty, Madhya Pradesh. Buff sandstone relief, 51.5 x 33.5 x 10 cm. Victoria & Albert Museum, London.

masterpieces in the later years of the fifth century. In painting we have the frescoes of Ajanta and Bagh.

Owing to the destruction wrought by iconoclast Muslim armies who overran and held in strength almost every part of the Gupta Empire, few remains of the period exist above ground, except in out-of-the-way localities, and our present knowledge of Gupta art is largely the result of excavation. One of the surprises of recent exploration has been the discovery of many large Buddhist monasteries at Sarnath dating from the fifth and sixth centuries. The sculpture of the period is mainly Buddhist and Hindu.

In the fifth century were built the earliest stone buildings that have survived. They are chiefly tiny shrines situated in out-of-the-way places. These small shrines are really the prototypes of much of the architecture of the great cave temples at Ajanta and Ellora. All the known examples are Brahmanical. At Ajanta the Buddhist rock-cut Vihara, which was originally nothing but a large pillared hall with cells for dwelling purposes leading into it on the three inner sides, was converted to ritual purposes by cutting a shrine exactly corresponding to the Gupta structural shrines in the back wall.

A temple at Deogarh, in the Jhansi District, is adorned with sculptures of exceptionally good quality in panels inserted in the plinth and walls, which may date from the first half of the sixth century. That region probably escaped the Hun troubles owing to its remote situation. A panel on the eastern façade, representing Shiva in the garb of an ascetic attended by another yogi and various heavenly beings hovering in the air, may claim a place among the best efforts of Indian sculpture.

Among the numerous excellent sculptures of Gupta age, disclosed by recent excavations at Sarnath, the most pleasing is the seated Buddha in white sandstone. The deer park at Sarnath having been the place where the Wheel of the Law was first turned, or the doctrine of the Buddhist way of salvation was first publicly preached by Gautama Buddha, his effigy is naturally represented with the fingers in the symbolic position (*mudra*) associated by canonical rules with the act commemorated. The wheel symbolizing the Law and the five adoring disciples to whom it was first preached are depicted on the pedestal. The beautifully decorated halo characteristic of the period is in marked contrast with the severely plain halos of the Kushan age.

The unique copper colossus of Buddha, weighing nearly a ton, more closely akin to the Sarnath than to the Mathura image, the robes being almost smooth, with the folds marked very faintly. The transparency of the garments is clearly marked. The statue may be dated early fifth century. The existence of the Sultanganj Buddha is good evidence of Indian proficiency in metallurgy at the beginning of the fifth century.

▶ *Sadashiva. The supreme expression of Shiva's divine form, each face expressing a contrasting mood or sentiment. On the left is Shiva as the fearsome form of his aghora aspect, opposite are the soft features of his feminine nature, Vamadeva-Parvati, and in the centre is the divinely calm and meditative Shiva as the supreme yogi Mahadeva,* c. 550 C.E., Early Chalukya dynasty. Rock-cut relief, 610 m. Elephanta, Maharashtra.

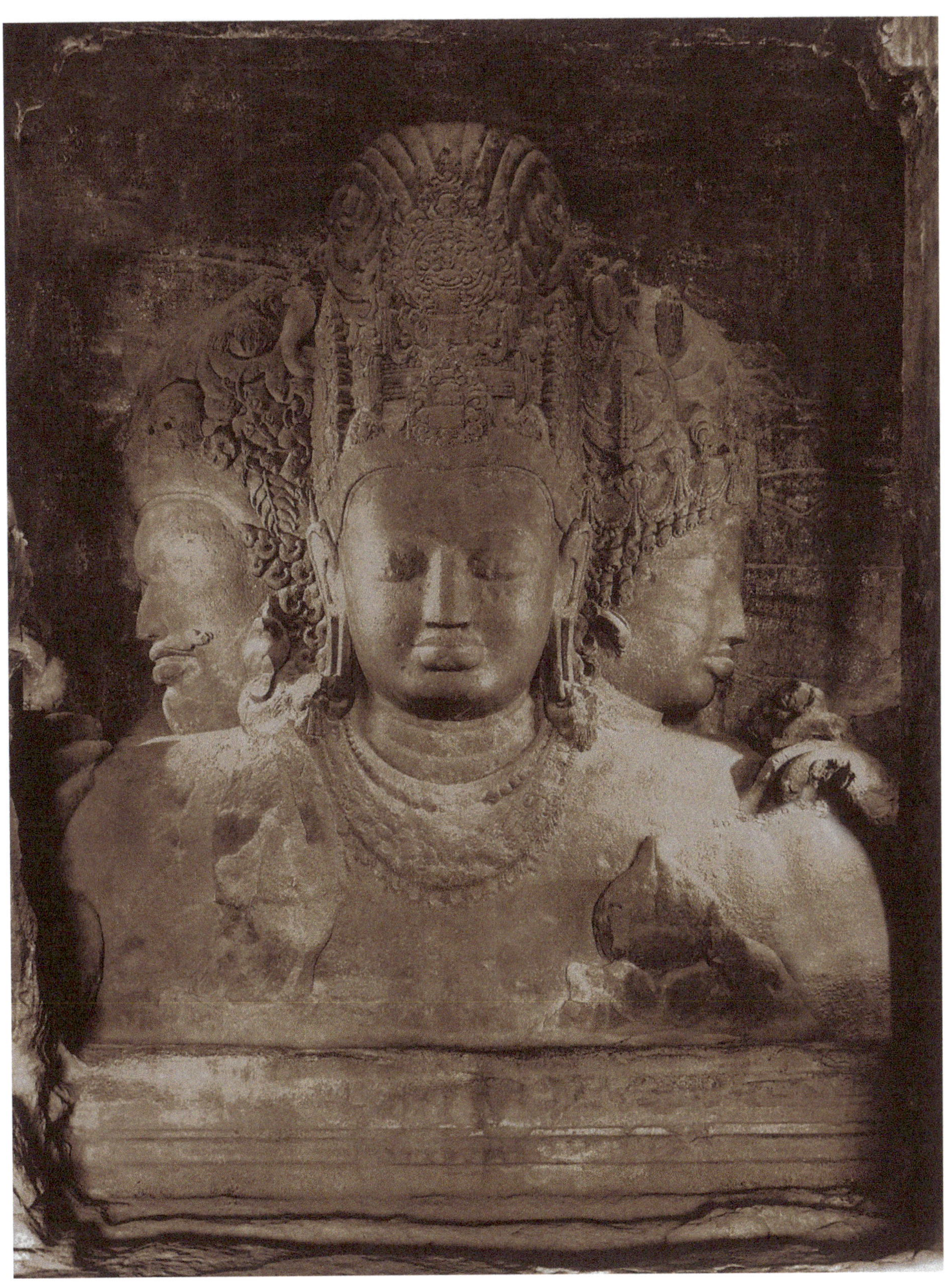

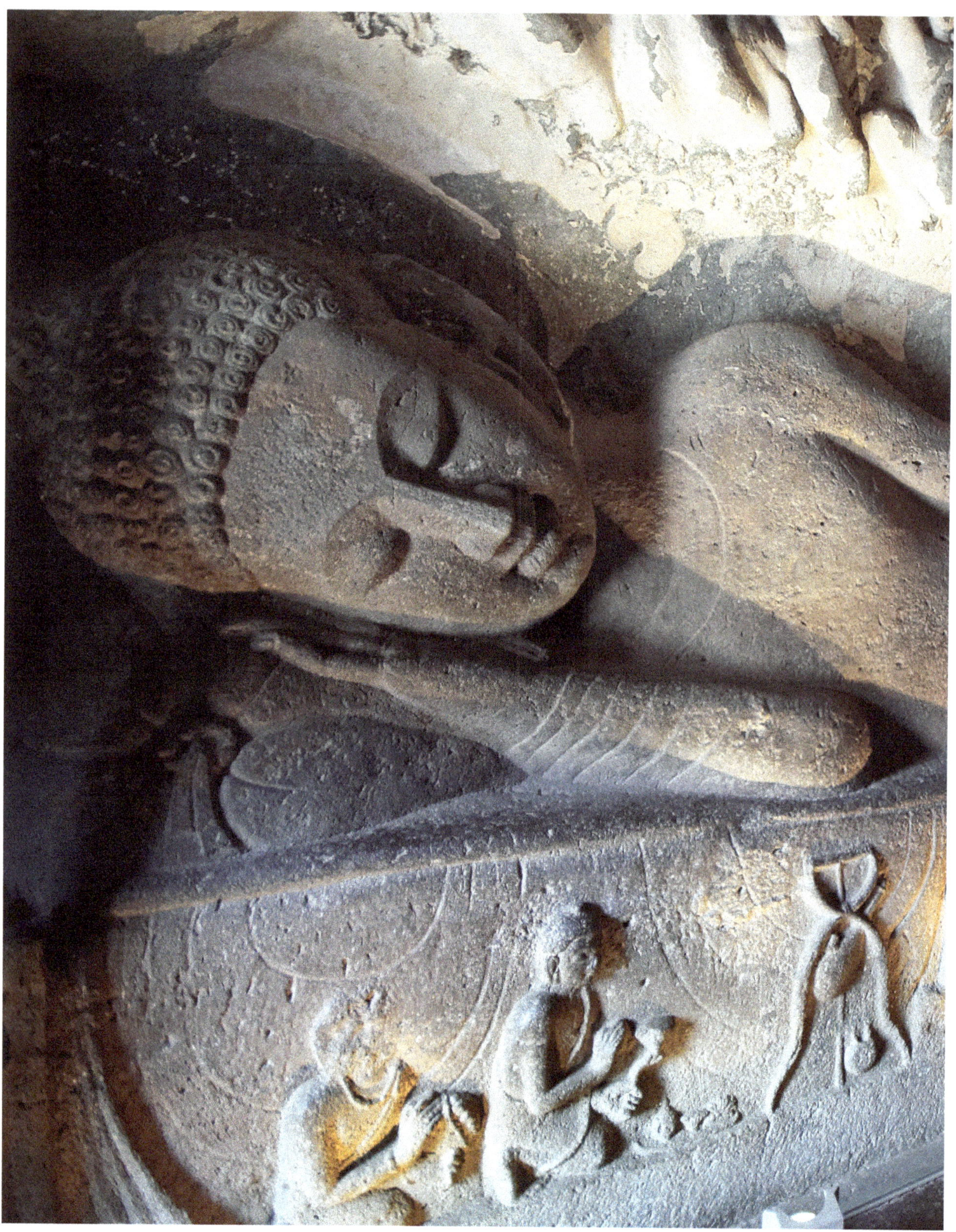

THE MEDIEVAL PERIOD IN THE NORTH OF INDIA

Architecture: Cave-Temples and Temples

The most characteristic and distinctive sculptures of Gupta age occur in Northern India.

The numerous sculptures in Cave XXVI include a gigantic recumbent Dying Buddha, seven meters in length, bearing a general resemblance to the fifth-century image at Kasia in the Gorakhpur District. The most notable sculpture on the walls is the large and crowded composition representing the Temptation of Buddha. The subject is also treated at Ajanta in fresco.

In Cave I, supposed to be the latest of the completed excavations, a great quantity of rich sculpture exists, dealing chiefly with incidents in the lives of Buddha. A scene depicting the chase of the wild bull is praised as being 'spiritedly carved'.

The principal cave, No. III, contains many columns most elaborately decorated with figure sculpture as well as complex patterns. On certain of these columns a sixteen-sided portion is carved with sixteen scenes. They seem intended to picture the 'Drunkard's Progress'. Two persons are represented sitting together, apparently drinking in the friendliest way, then staggering along, then dancing with their backs to each other, then quarrelling; one is being dragged along helpless between two men, and so on in successive panels.

Certain groups of kneeling worshippers in the same excavation are extremely curious. The mode of hairdressing has quite an Egyptian appearance. At Ajanta much of the sculpture is reminiscent of the Gupta fifth-century temples. In the later caves the work is definitely medieval, being based on the iconography of the time. The grotesque animals with foliated tails, and many motives based on jewelry designs, distinguish it from the Gupta. The cave sculptures of interest range in date from the sixth to the eighth century.

The famous caves on the island of Elephanta in Bombay Harbour are Shiva and usually supposed to date from the eighth century. The colossal sculptures are most imposing and effective when viewed in the recesses of the caverns. The first of the two specimens is the favorite subject of the

◄ Parinirvana: the final nirvana, when Buddha, upon death, attained complete awakening (bodhi), end of 6th cenury C.E., Gupta period. Rock-cut relief of left wall, length: 707 cm. Ajanta caves (Cave XXVI), near Aurangabad, Maharashtra.

marriage of Shiva with Parvati; and the second is the representation of Shiva as the Great Ascetic. The most imposing of the Elephanta sculptures is the gigantic *Trimurti* or Trinity, which is the first thing, discerned as the eyes become accustomed to the gloom.

Throughout India, except Buddhist remains, there is hardly anything standing which can be dated earlier than 450 C.E. No early examples of civil architecture exist. After the date named, Buddhist structures become scarce. The styles of Indian architecture in the medieval period, therefore, must be deduced from Brahmanical and Jain temples, or from the buildings represented in the Ajanta frescoes.

When it first comes to Indian architecture, our knowledge is full-grown and complete. The earliest specimens betray no signs of tentative effort, and in no case is it possible to trace the progressive evolution of a given style from rude beginnings. The extensive destruction of ancient monuments, especially those built of brick, supplies a partial explanation. The more fundamental explanation is probably to be found in the assumption that all the Indian styles are derived from prototypes constructed in timber, bamboos, and other perishable materials.

In the crowd of varieties two leading styles of temple architecture – the Northern or Indo-Aryan, and the Southern or Dravidian – may be readily distinguished. The two styles may more simply be denominated Northern and Southern. The Aryavarta, or Northern style, examples of

which to the south of the Narmada are rare, is characterized by the bulging steeple with curvilinear vertical ribs, placed over the sanctuary, and frequently reproduced on other parts of the building. Miniature repetitions of the form are often used with good effect as decorations of the steeples themselves.

The best early examples are found at Bhubaneswar in the Puri District, where the temples, numbering several hundred, illustrate the history of the style from the ninth to the thirteenth century. The earliest specimens have steeples comparatively low and squat, but pleasing to an eye which has become accustomed to the design. The porch is a walled chamber with a low, massive roof. The combination of vertical and horizontal lines is skillfully arranged so as to give dignity to buildings of moderate height. The Bhubaneswar group of temples stands first in importance among the examples of the Aryavarta style.

The most renowned achievement of the vigorous Orissan school of architects is the temple of the Sun, a UNESCO World Heritage Site at Konark on the coast, known to sailors as the Black Pagoda, in order to distinguish it from the White Pagoda, or temple of Jagannath at Puri. The remains of the main steeple, never completed, which had been overwhelmed long ago by the drifting sand, have been lately exposed by excavation. The porch,

▶ *Two figures with drum*, late 6ᵗʰ century C.E. Sandstone. Ellora caves (Cave XV), Aurangabad, Maharashtra.

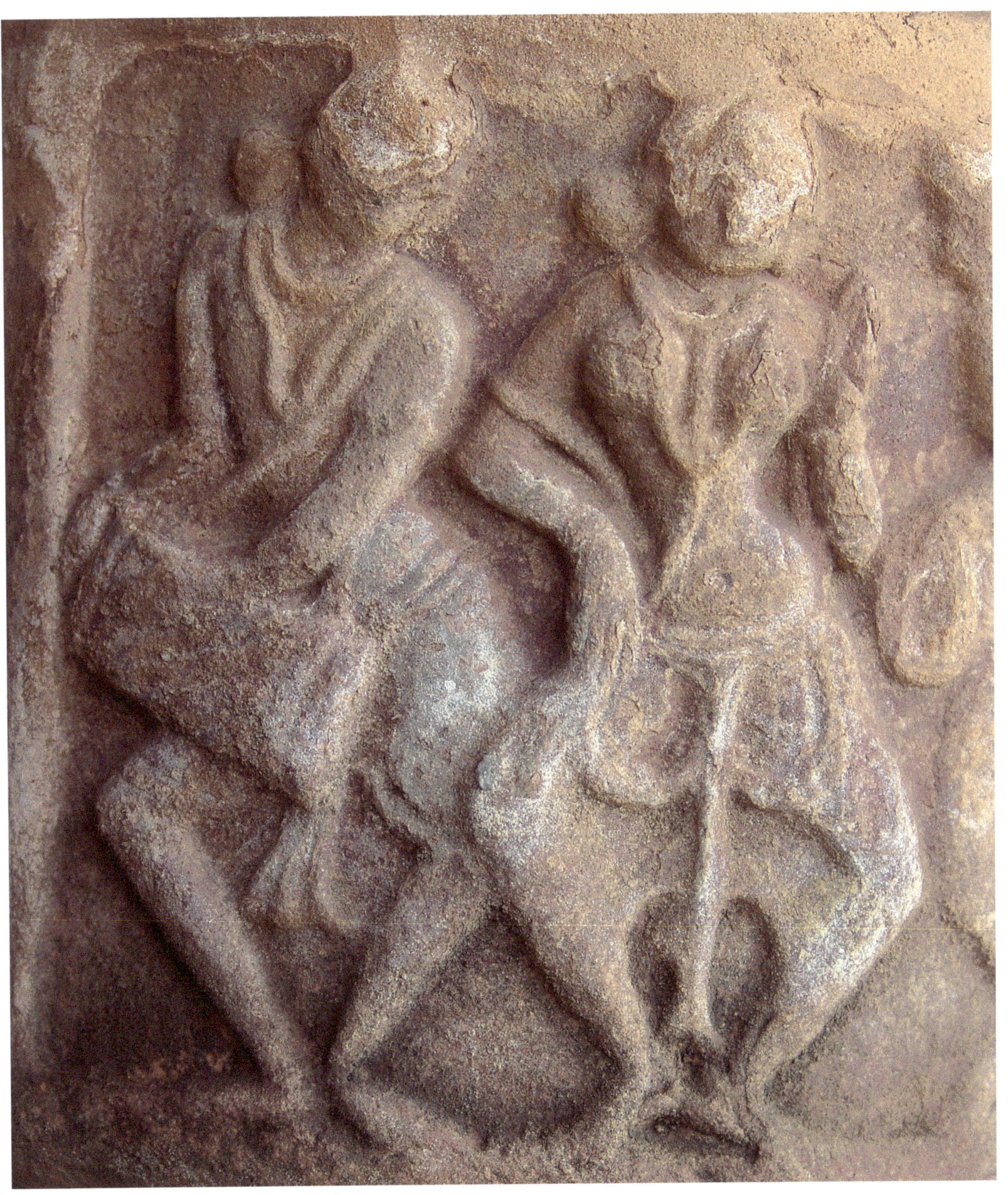

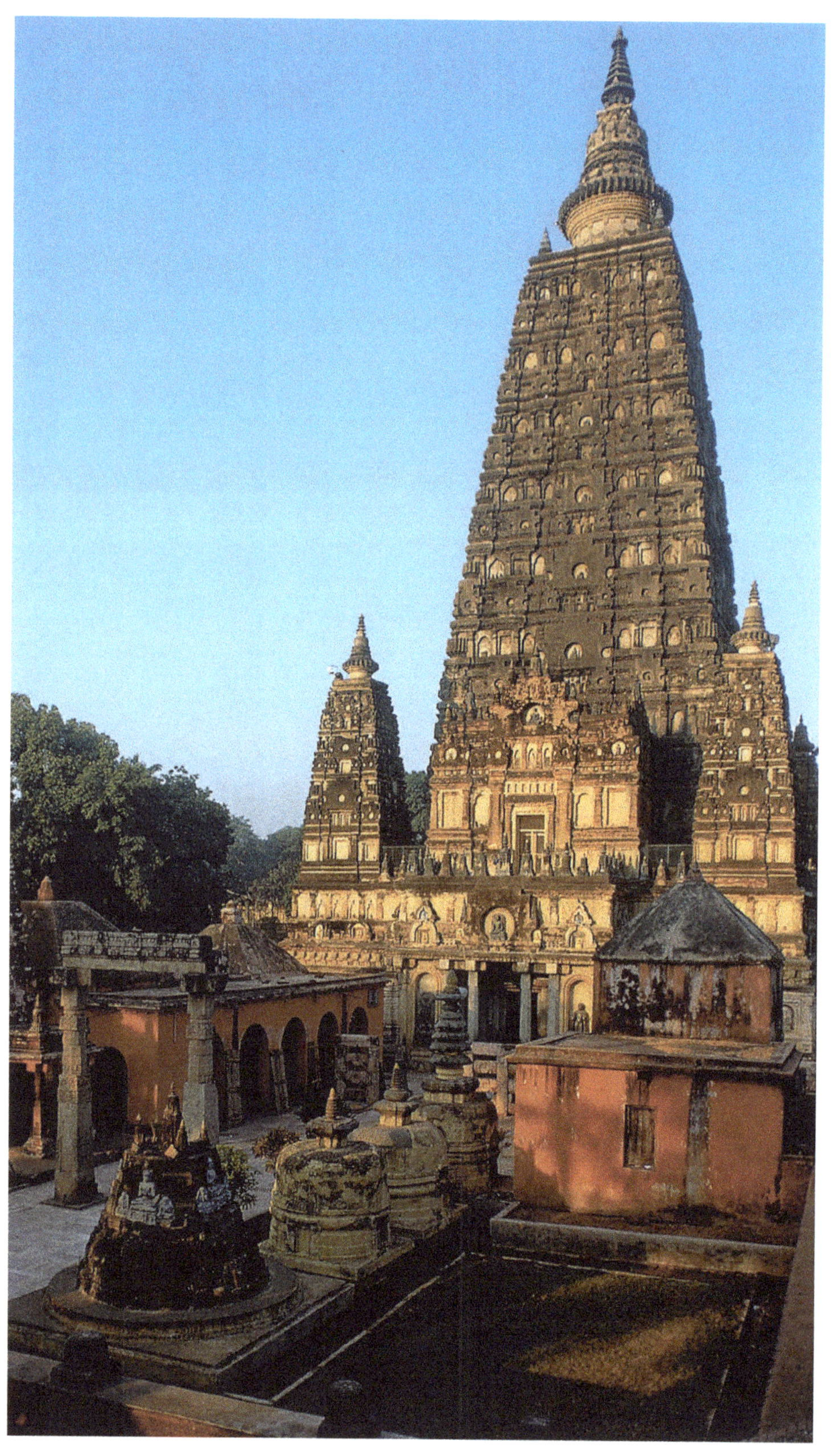

which stands practically perfect, is covered by a beautifully designed pyramidal roof.

There are many fine brick temples in the Central Provinces, the finest of which is at Sirpur. These temples have massively carved stone doorposts, lintels, and pillars. There is reason to believe that the transition from wooden to stone architecture was made through brick, and that the scarcity of old brick buildings is due to the facility with which the material could be utilized for other constructions. The decorations of brick buildings were carried out in terracotta, and carved as well as molded bricks were used.

Sculpture: Medieval and Modern Objects

The spirit of medieval sculpture is chiefly expressed in Brahmanical and Buddhist works, which alike exalt the ascetic ideal and reflect the teachings of Puranic and Tantric literature. The ascetic Buddha no longer appears as the sympathetic human teacher instructing his disciples in the Good Law. His image is now generally made to conform to the ideal of the passionless yogi, as described in the Bhagavad-Gita.

◀ *Mahabodhi Temple*, 250 B.C.E./5ᵗʰ-6ᵗʰ century C.E., Maurya dynasty (Ashoka)/late Gupta period. Brick. Bodh Gaya, Bihar.

▼ *Parasuramesvara Temple*, 7ᵗʰ century B.C.E. Stone, height: 13 m. Bhubaneswar, Orissa.

▼ *Konark Sun Temple*, 8ᵗʰ century, Ganga dynasty. Stone, form of the chariot of Surya (Arka), the sun god, Konark, Orissa.

Another dominant note in medieval sculpture is struck by the Endeavour of the artists to express violent superhuman emotion or demoniac passion, as represented by the whirling dances of Shiva, the strivings of Marichi, the struggling of Ravana beneath his mountain load, and many other iconographic compositions. Multitudes of sculptures are simply the formal images of innumerable gods and goddesses.

The first part of the medieval period is illustrated by the great cave temples of Ajanta, Badami, and Ellora. Apart from the great shrines of Rajasthan, Khajuraho, and Mount Abu, late medieval sculpture falls into two main territorial divisions, namely, 1) Bihar, both North and South, with certain adjoining districts of Bengal and the Agra Provinces, which collectively formed the dominions of the Pala dynasty for more than four centuries until the date of the Islamic conquest; and 2) Orissa, on the coast of the Bay of Bengal.

The Pala kings having been devout Buddhists to the last, Buddhism continued to be the dominant religion in their territories and the Buddhist monasteries of Bihar, especially the wealthy foundation at Nalanda, were crowded with thousands of monks, who cultivated with success the arts required for the decoration of the sacred buildings. In consequence, a large proportion of the sculpture in Bihar and the neighboring regions is Buddhist. The later Buddhism was of the *Mahayana* or 'Great Vehicle' kind, delighting in the use of images, and closely related to Hinduism.

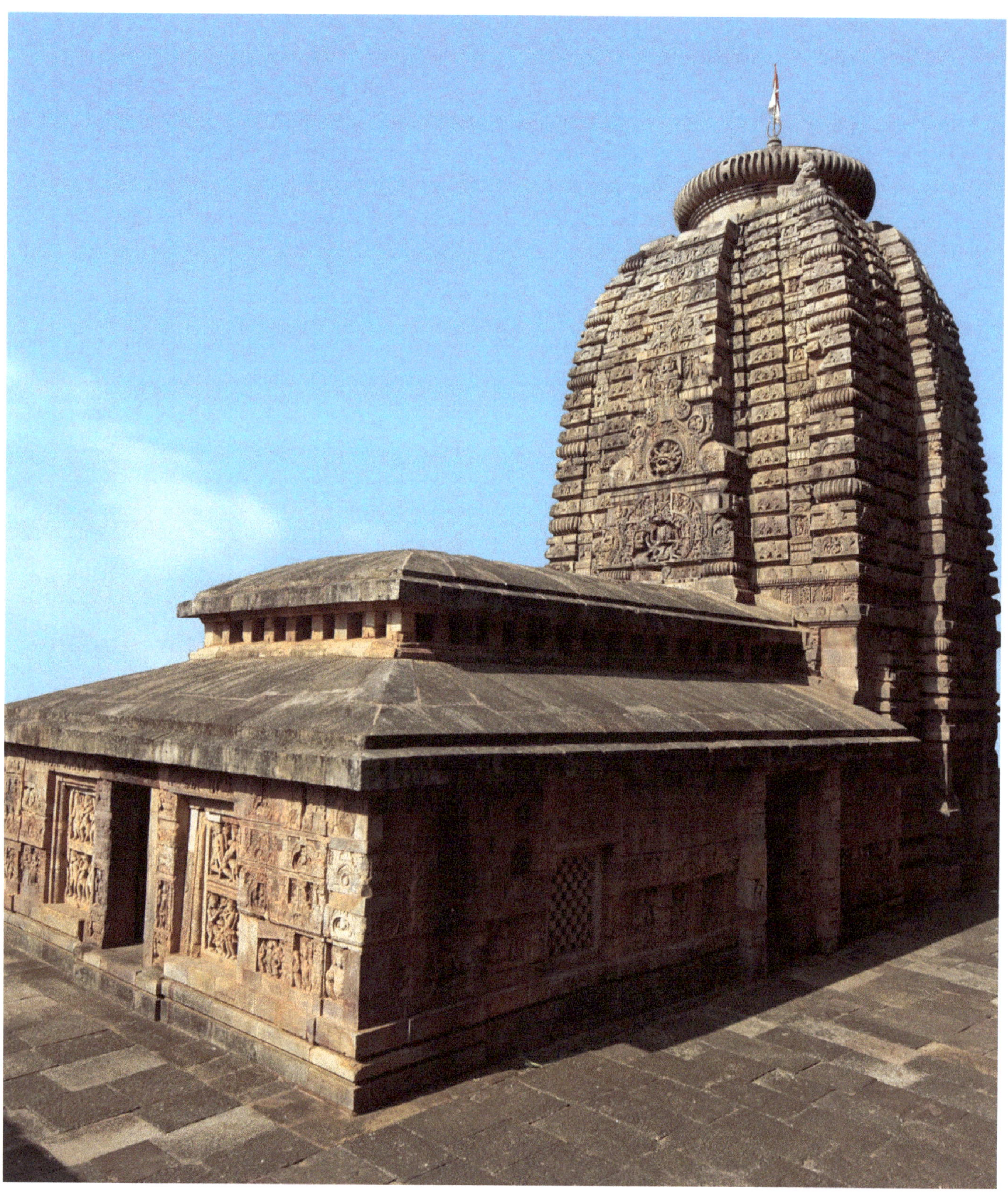

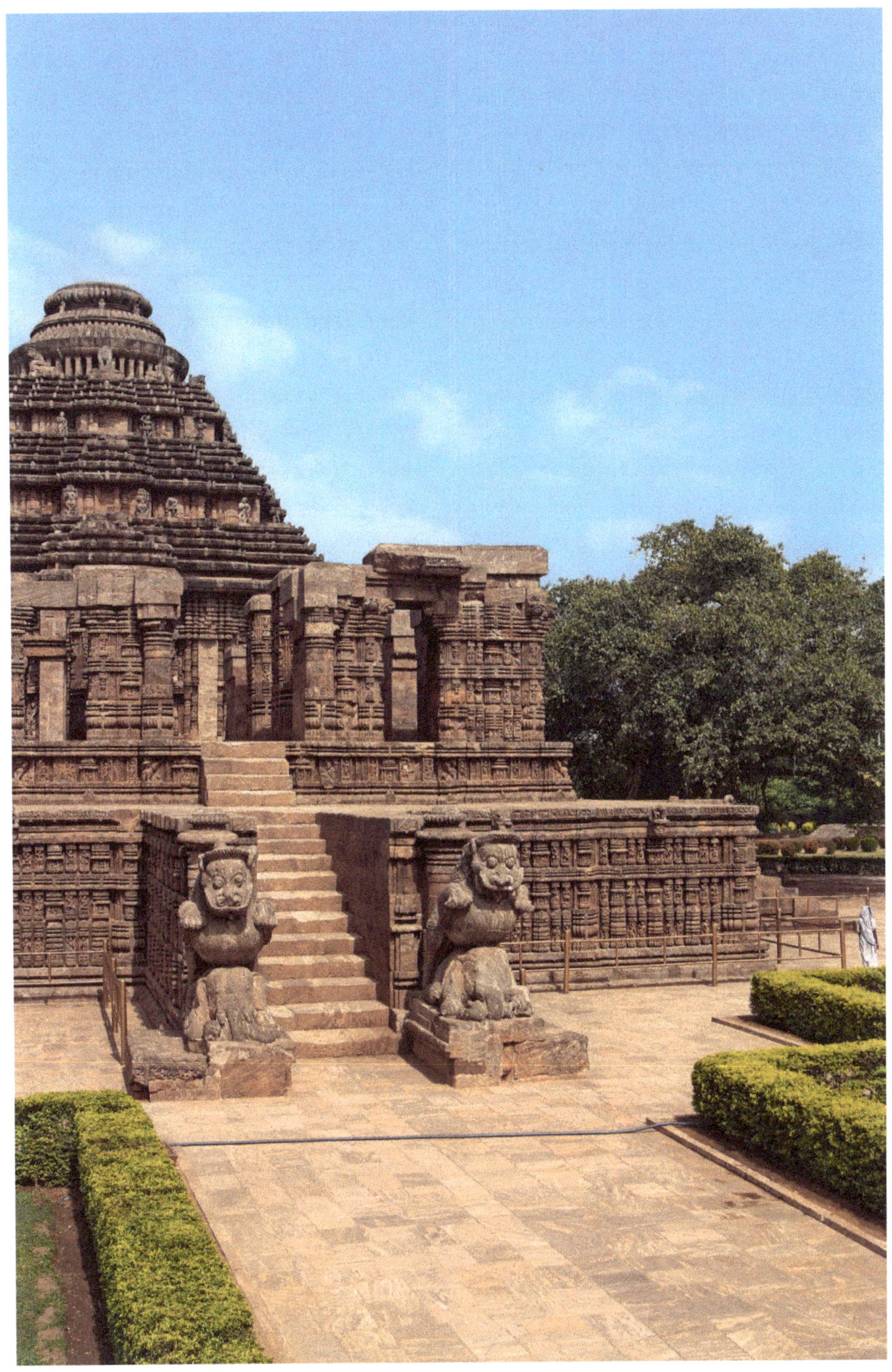

During the first half of the seventh century, the Buddhists of Orissa outnumbered the Brahmanical Hindus, but notwithstanding that fact, Buddhist sculpture is rare in the province, and the extant specimens, often of a high class, are mainly Brahmanical. From the point of view of the historian of art religious distinctions in the medieval period are unimportant, sculptors making use of the style of their own age and country.

In Bihar, the Muslim onslaught at the close of the twelfth century overthrew Buddhism suddenly, and scattered all over India those few monks who survived the indiscriminate massacres committed by the iconoclast armies of Islam. The rich monasteries of Sarnath near Varanasi soon shared the fate of the communities in Bihar, and layers of ashes in the ruins testify to this day the violence of the conquerors.

One of the best and most characteristic examples of Bihar sculpture is the large group of the sun god and his attendants now in the Victoria and Albert Museum, which is in nearly perfect preservation. The god is represented standing in a lotus-shaped chariot drawn by seven horses, and driven by the legless Aruna, the Dawn. The artist has concentrated his attention on the effigy of the god, reducing the chariot, horses, and charioteer to the position of minor accessories, in such a way that a casual spectator might fail to perceive their significance. The body of the principal figure is carefully modeled with considerable regard to realism, and the same commendation may be bestowed on the two female attendants with fly-whisks.

The Tower of Victory at Chittoor in Rajasthan, built in the fifteenth century to commemorate the military successes of a local chieftain, is covered from top to bottom, inside and out, with an infinite multitude of images, representing all the denizens of the Hindu pantheon, with their names attached, and constituting an 'illustrated dictionary of Hindu mythology'. It is invaluable as a key to Brahmanical iconography, but is not likely to contribute much to the history of art.

Certain relief sculptures at the Mokalji temple on the famous rock of Chittoor have high merit as works of art. The temple, originally erected in the eleventh century, was reconstructed in the fifteenth century during the reign of Mokalji (1428-1438 C.E.). The bas-reliefs, sixteen in number, are carved on octagonal bands, eight scenes on each pillar. The first scene on the southern column of the pair depicts five human figures, one of the former represents a woman carrying a water jar on her head, and a man standing before her with hands joined in an attitude of adoration. This sculpture, along with the others of this set, is remarkable for the elaborate detail and technical excellence of its workmanship, the woman's hair being most minutely delineated. The third carving is very well modeled and proportioned, and depicts two standing figures, male and female. The fifth scene is filled with vigorous action, and consists of a musical festival; six male figures play musical instruments.

▶ *Kandariya Mahadeva Temple*, c. 1050, Chandella dynasty. Stone, height: 31 m. Khajuraho, Madhya Pradesh.

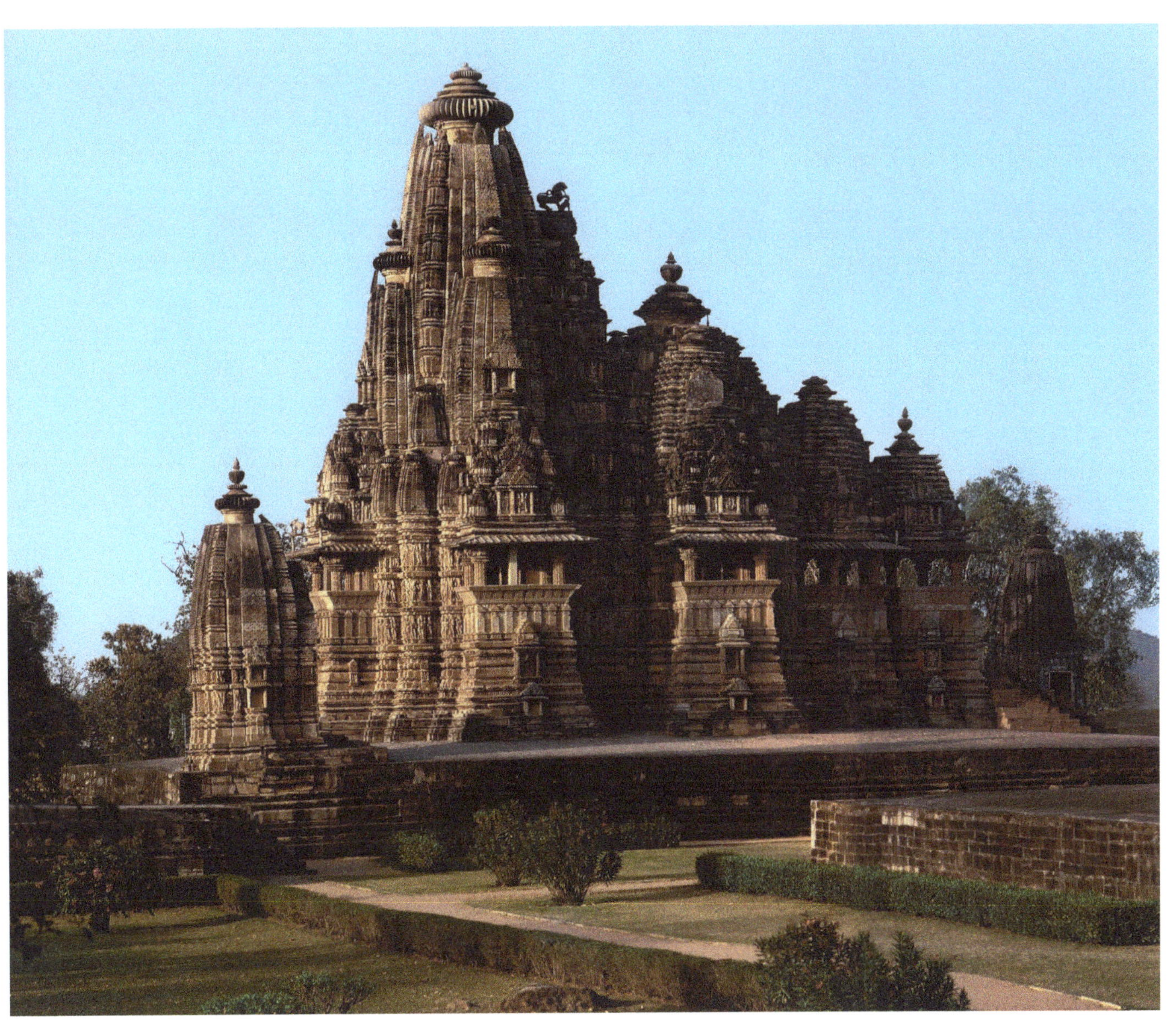

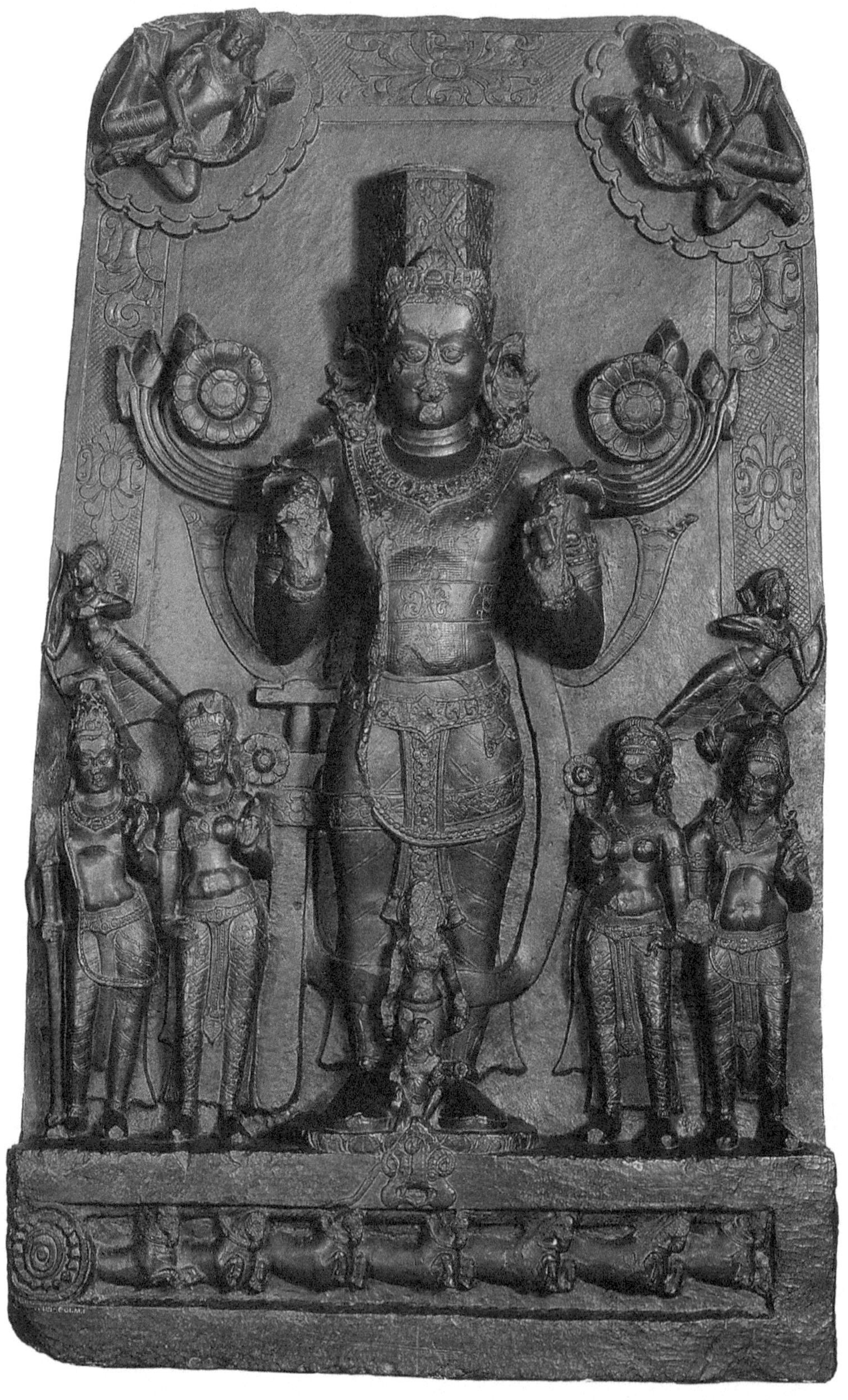

The sixth and last figure of this interesting group is seen full to the front, blowing a flute in a very animated position as if he were dancing.

On the northern column of the seventh scene is in all probability the most interesting of the whole series, and in its half a dozen figures gives us both a duel and an execution. The upper pair of men fight with shields and sabers, and their armor, even the bosses on their shields, are most carefully delineated. The lower portion of this comprehensive scene shows a pair of kneeling figures bound hand and foot, while an executioner holds his knife to the neck of the male figure; but the female with him may be a mere witness, though it is pretty clear that she awaits her turn for immolation.

Painting: The Early Schools (Ajanta Caves)

Few people realize that the art of painting in India and Sri Lanka has a long history, illustrated by extant examples ranging over a period exceeding two thousand years, and that during the so-called Dark Ages the Indian painters attained a degree of proficiency not matched in Europe before the fourteenth century. Unfortunately,

◀ Surya holding a flowering lotus in both hands. The sun god travels through the sky on a chariot drawn by seven horses, seen on the base of the sculpture. At his feet is his charioteer Aruna, and his consort, and he is attended by the personifications of earth and air. Celestial archers drive off the hosts of the night (personifications of the stars) and bring the light of day, early 10th century, Pala dynasty, Bihar. Black Basalt (carboniferous shale), 142 x 86 x 9 cm. Victoria & Albert Museum, London.

the incompleteness of the record compels the historian to leave many gaps in his narrative. The widest gap lies between the close of the Ajanta series in the seventh and the introduction of the Indo-Persian style by Akbar in the sixteenth century. Some evidence is furnished by remains of ancient painting from the second century B.C.E.; which, even in their present fragmentary state, enables the modern critic to appraise the style of the early Indian artists, and to recognize the just claim of the art of India to take high rank among the ancient schools of painting.

The oldest Indian pictures are found in the Jogimara Cave of the Ramgarh Hill in the District of Uttar Pradesh. These pictures, apparently executed in the customary Indian method of fresco are divided into concentric circles by bands of red and yellow, sometimes enriched with a geometrical design, these circles seemingly being again subdivided into panels. They probably date from the second century B.C.E. As regards technique, the designs are painted usually in red, but occasionally in black, on a white ground. The outlines of the human and animal figures are drawn in black. Clothing is white with red outlines, hair is black, and eyes are white. Yellow appears in the dividing bands only, and blue does not seem to occur.

The story of the art of painting in India is continued by the celebrated frescoes of the Ajanta caves in the west, ranging in date from about 50 C.E. to about the sixth century, They constitute the most important mass of ancient painting extant in the world, Pompeii only excepted. The twenty-nine caves are 'excavated in the face of an almost perpendicular scarp of rock about 26 meters high, admirably adapted for a monastic retreat, is situated southwest from Phardapur.

The bulk of the paintings unquestionably must be assigned to the time of the great Chalukya kings (550-642 C.E.) and of the earlier Vakataka kings of Berar. A Vakataka inscription exists in Cave XVI. It is unlikely that any can have been executed later than the second date named, when Pulakesin II was dethroned and presumably killed by the Pallava king of the South, ardent worshippers of Shiva.

The Indian practice of wall painting at Ajanta, is in fact a combination of tempera with fresco. The hydraulic nature of Indian lime, or *chunam*, makes it possible to keep a surface moist for a longer time than in Europe, and the Indian practice of toweling the work unknown in Europe produced a closer and more intimate liaison between the color and the lime, and a more durable and damp-resisting face than the open texture of European fresco.

The subjects of the pictures are almost exclusively Buddhist and include numerous figures of Buddha and representations of sacred objects and symbols. The more complex compositions deal with either the incidents of the life of Gautama Buddha or those related in the Jataka stories, which narrates the events of his former births. In Cave X the tale of the six-tusked elephant and a few other legends may be identified with more or less certainty.

The smaller panels are ornamented with designs as varied and graceful as they are fanciful. Some with grotesque little figures, rich in humor and quaintly dressed in Persian turbans, coats, and striped stockings; gamboling amid fruits and flowers; dancing, drinking, or playing upon instruments; or chattering together; some with animals combined with the lotus, drawn with remarkable fidelity and action.

In the sixth-century Cave XVII, the charming floral designs combined with human figures on the panels of the pillars are closely related to the slightly earlier sculptured work on the Garhwa pillars in northern India. The *kirttimukha* grinning faces are common throughout medieval Indian art.

The earliest works are certain paintings in Caves IX and X, closely related to the Sanchi sculptures. The figures of Buddha painted on the pillars of Cave X are probably the next in date, and should be assigned to the fifth century. The nimbus and draperies recall early Christian art and the sculptures of Gandhara.

Cave XVII may fairly be considered the most interesting of the series. No less than sixty-one

▶ *Portrait of King Narasimha (1238-1264), the architect of the Sun Temple at Konark, Orissa, receiving spiritual instruction from his chief priest, who is seated to the right. The figures are treated hierarchically, with the priest represented in a larger scale to define the correct guru-pupil relationship*, mid-13th century, Ganga dynasty, Konark, Orissa. Black Basalt (carboniferous shale), 78.5 x 43 x 23 cm. Victoria & Albert Museum, London.

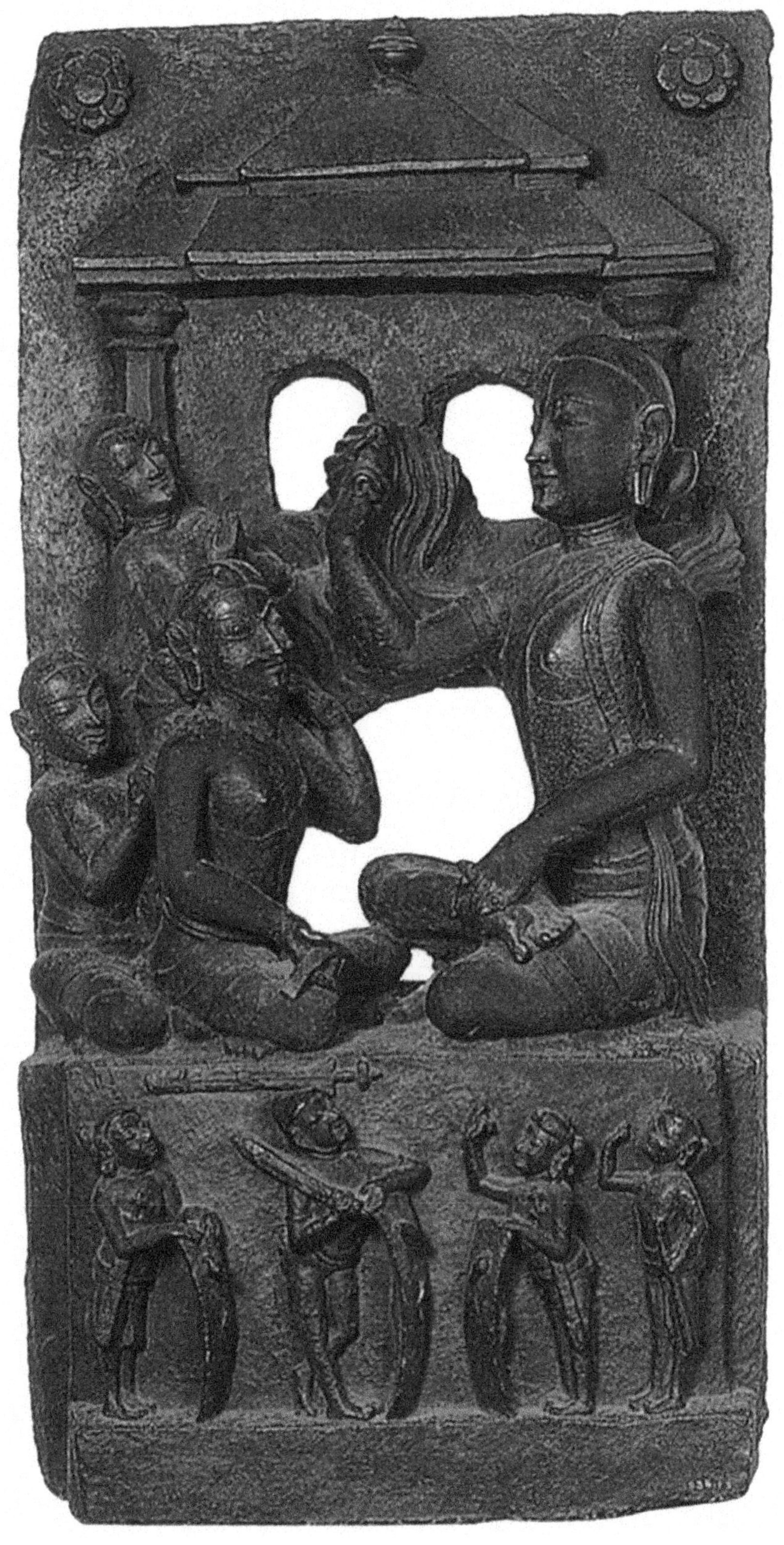

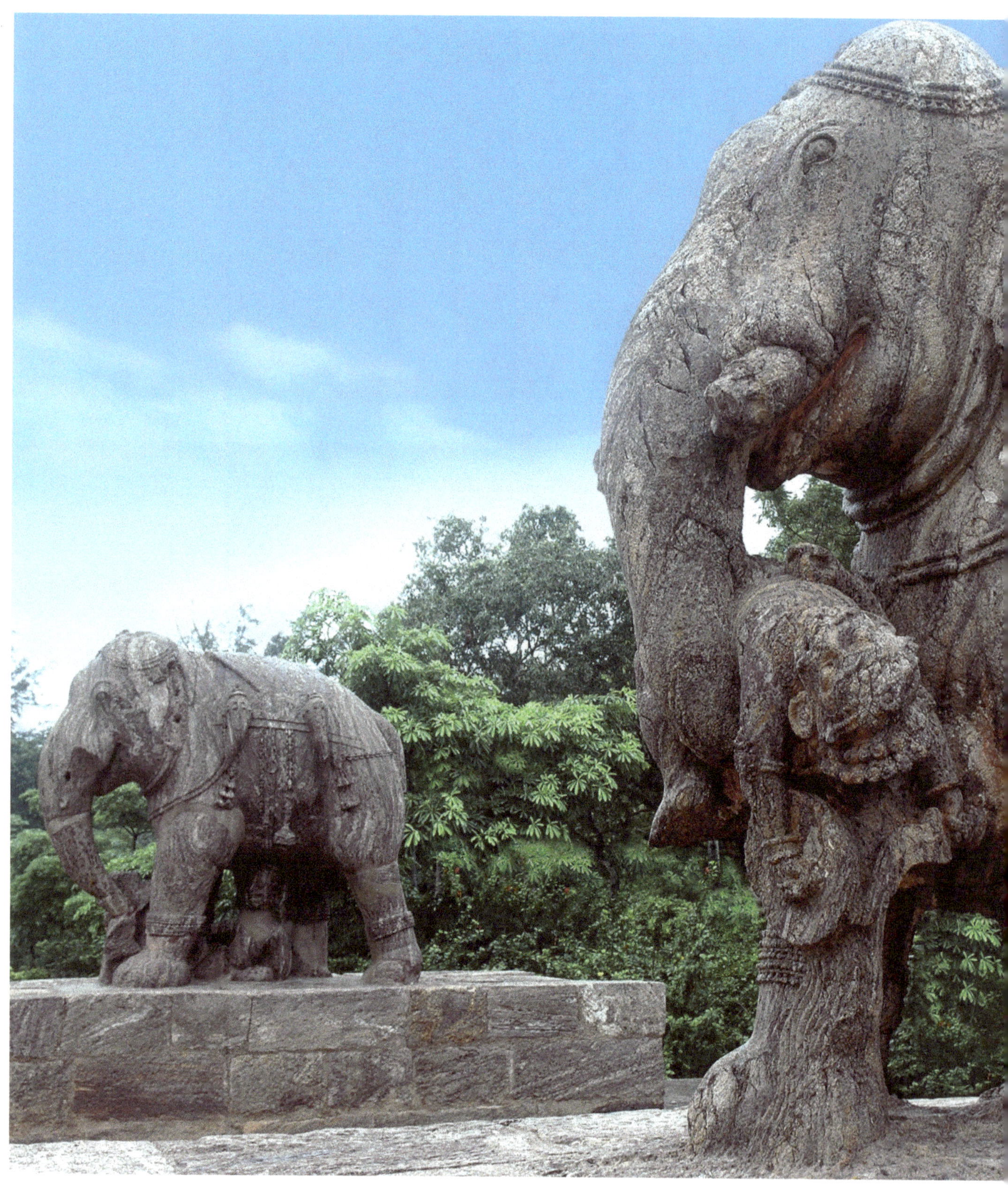

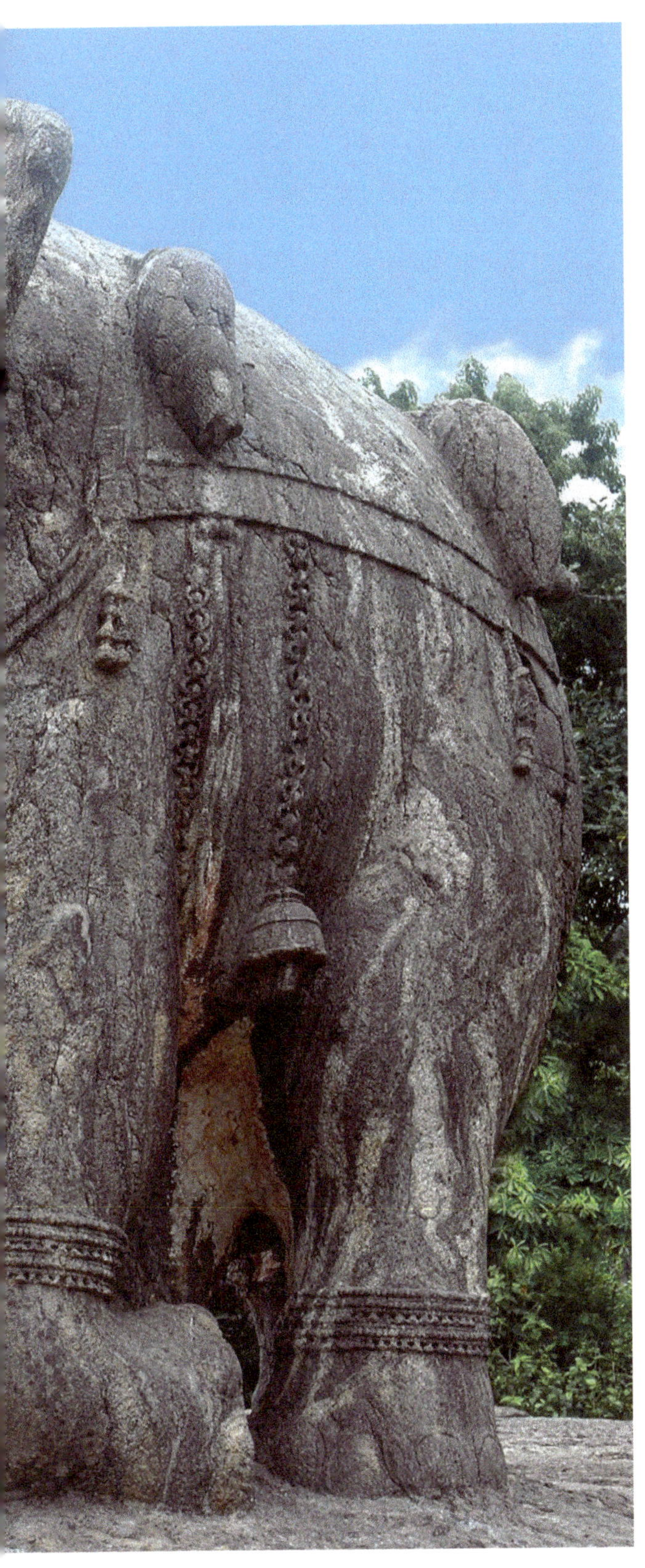

distinct scenes are described. The two largest pictures are so excessively crowded with figures and so deficient in unity of composition that they cannot be presented satisfactorily except on an enormous scale. The representation in the left end of the verandah of the Buddhist Wheel of Life, commonly miscalled the Zodiac, is interesting rather as an illustration of popular Buddhist teaching in the sixth century than as a work of art. The individual figures in Caves I and II, No. I, are probably the latest of the completed works are remarkable for clever drawing, the artist having apparently gone out of his way to invent especially difficult poses. A woman prostrating herself, and snake-hooded Nagas, or water sprites, are good examples of such tours de force. The woman standing, with her left leg bent up, is capital, the feet being as well drawn as the hands.

Further, in Cave XVII there are three paintings by one hand, very different from all the rest. They are (1) a hunt of lions and black buck; (2) a hunt of elephants; and (3) an elephant salaaming in a king's court. These pictures are composed in a light and shade scheme which can scarcely be paralleled in Italy before the seventeenth century. They are nearly monochrome, except that the foliage and grass are dull green. The animals, horses, elephants, dogs and black buck are extremely well drawn.

◄ *Two Elephant Sculptures (extension part of the Konark Sun Temple)*, 13th century, Ganga dynasty.
Sandstone. Konark, Orissa.

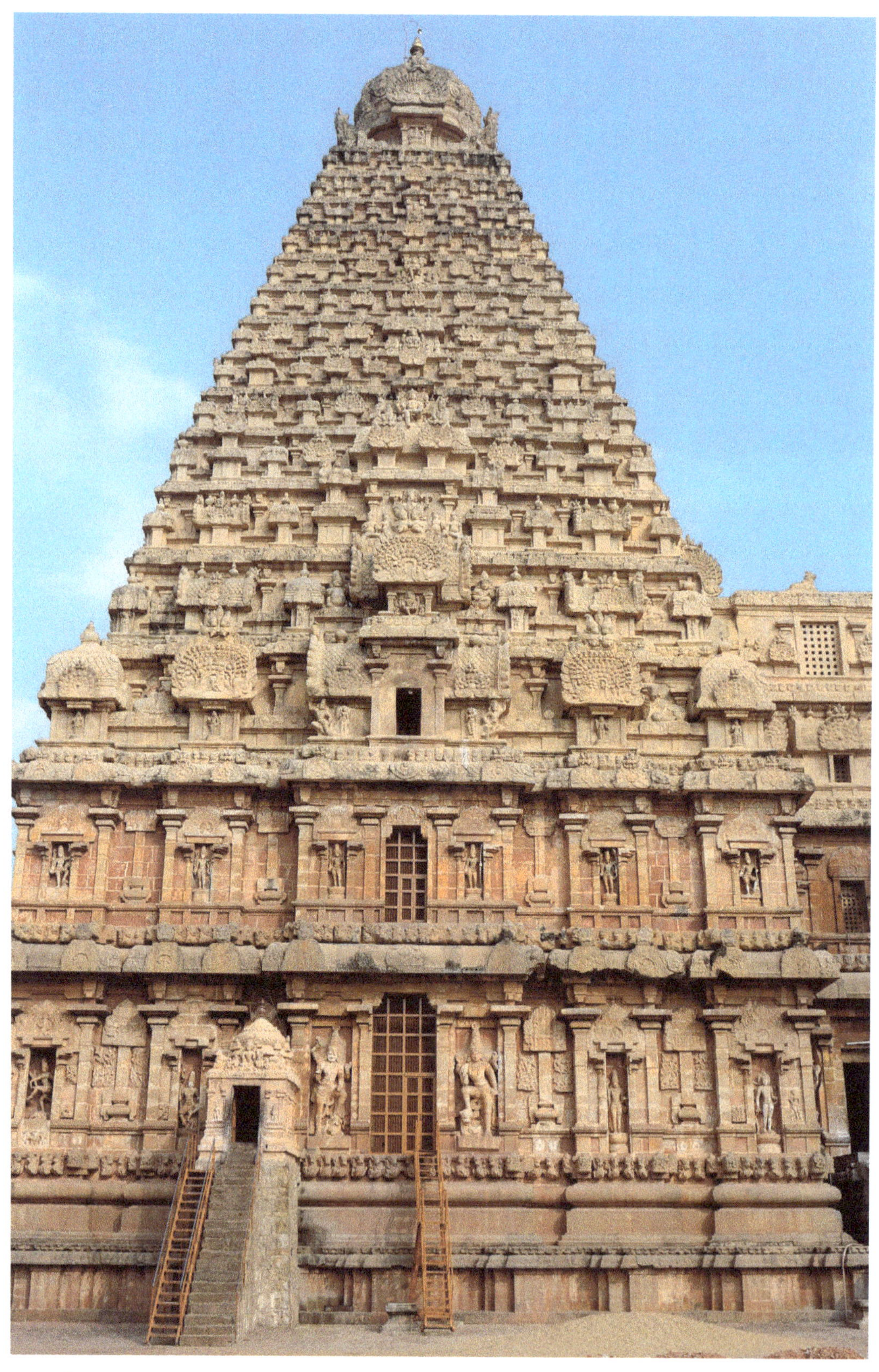

THE MEDIEVAL PERIOD IN THE SOUTH OF INDIA

Architecture

If the Dravidian or Southern style of architecture is sharply distinguished from the Northern by the fact that its spire is straight-lined and pyramidal in form, divided into stories by horizontal bands, and surmounted by either a barrel roof or a dome. The central shrine originally stood alone, but in later times it was enclosed in an immense walled court, usually including numerous subsidiary temples.

The history of the style begins in the seventh century with the Dharmaraja Ratha, the earliest of the rock-cut rathas at Mahabalipuram, south of Madras, commonly known as the Seven Pagodas, which were excavated in the reigns of the Pallava kings of the South during the seventh century. The next stage in the development of the style is marked by the structural temples at Kanchipuram, the former Pallava capital.

◀ *Brihadisvara Temple*, 11th century, constructed by Raja Raja Chola. Granite, height: 66 m. Thanjavur, Tamil Nadu.

The gigantic South Indian temples, with vast quadrangular enclosures and lofty gopurams overtopping the central shrine, extend in date from the sixteenth century to the present day. The buildings at Madurai are of special interest because they can be dated closely, having been erected by Thirumalai Nayak, a local chieftain, who reigned from 1623 to 1659. The Madurai temple is a typical example. The corridors or cloisters connected with such temples are of wonderfully large dimensions and are filled with weird, fantastic sculpture.

The building stands on a terrace paved with large slabs. On this stands a frieze of elephants, following all the sinuosities of the plan containing not less than two thousand elephants, most of them with riders and trappings, sculptured as only an Oriental can represent the wisest of brutes.

Sculpture and Bronzes

The arts of sculpture and decorative carving in stone continued to be practiced in India to the south of the Narmada under the patronage of many dynasties throughout the medieval period, and even to this day are cultivated with considerable success. But, excepting certain Chola statuary of the eleventh century, which is excellent, the

Southern figure sculpture does not often attain high quality.

During the seventh century, the kings of the Pallava dynasty of Kanchipuram succeeded in making themselves the dominant power in southern India. The Pallava king named Mahendra-varman I (600-625), a great builder, is responsible for many rock-cut temples in the northern districts of Tamil Nadu. His son, Narasimha-varman I, the mightiest prince of his line, gave his name to Mahabalipuram. The great bas-relief at Mahabalipuram covers a sheet of rock 29 metres in length and 13 metres in breadth. Around a central figure, now missing, all creation, heavenly and earthly is gathered in worship.

The Cholas, who succeeded the Pallavas as the paramount power in the South, filled the principal places in the Tamil countries with their edifices, religious and secular, all richly sculptured. Rajaraja the Great (985-1018), the most famous king of a capable dynasty, extended his power over nearly the whole of the Madras Presidency, Sri Lanka, and a large part of Mysore. A king so powerful and wealthy naturally spent freely on building, and the world owes to him the temple at Thanjavur, his capital, the best designed of all the great South Indian temples.

In the year 1336, two Hindu brothers established a principality with its capital at Vijayanagar, which rapidly developed into an empire comprising all Southern India beyond the Kistna. The state attained the height of its prosperity early in the sixteenth century during the reign of Krishna Deva Raya, the contemporary of Henry VIII of England, who stoutly maintained the Hindu cause against the Muslim Sultans of the Deccan until 1565, when he was utterly defeated by the combined forces of the Islamic princes. The victors devoted their energies for five months to the deliberate destruction of the city.

One of the most notable of the ruins is the temple of Vishnu under the name Vitthalaswami, begun early in the sixteenth century. The great hall in front of the shrine rests on a richly sculptured basement, and its roof is supported by huge masses of granite, each consisting of a central pillar surrounded by detached shafts, figures mounted on demons, all cut from a single block of stone. The whole is carved with a boldness and expression of power nowhere surpassed in the buildings of its class, showing the extreme limit in florid magnificence to which the style advanced.

The capabilities of modern sculptors in the South are best proved by the decorations of the new palace in the town of Mysore. Skill is not confined to the members of any one caste, and the Maharaja was willing to employ capable men from any district. The material used is sometimes soapstone and sometimes stone of considerable hardness. The style throughout is frankly eclectic and imitative, and it is obvious that the artists have studied models of various periods and schools.

▶ *Sacred Temple water tank of Koviloor is used for the annual floating festival (teppotsava) when a portable icon is displayed on a floating pontoon and drawn around the tank, c. 11th century, Pandya dynasty, near Karaikudi. Laterite. Tinnevelly, Tamil Nadu.*

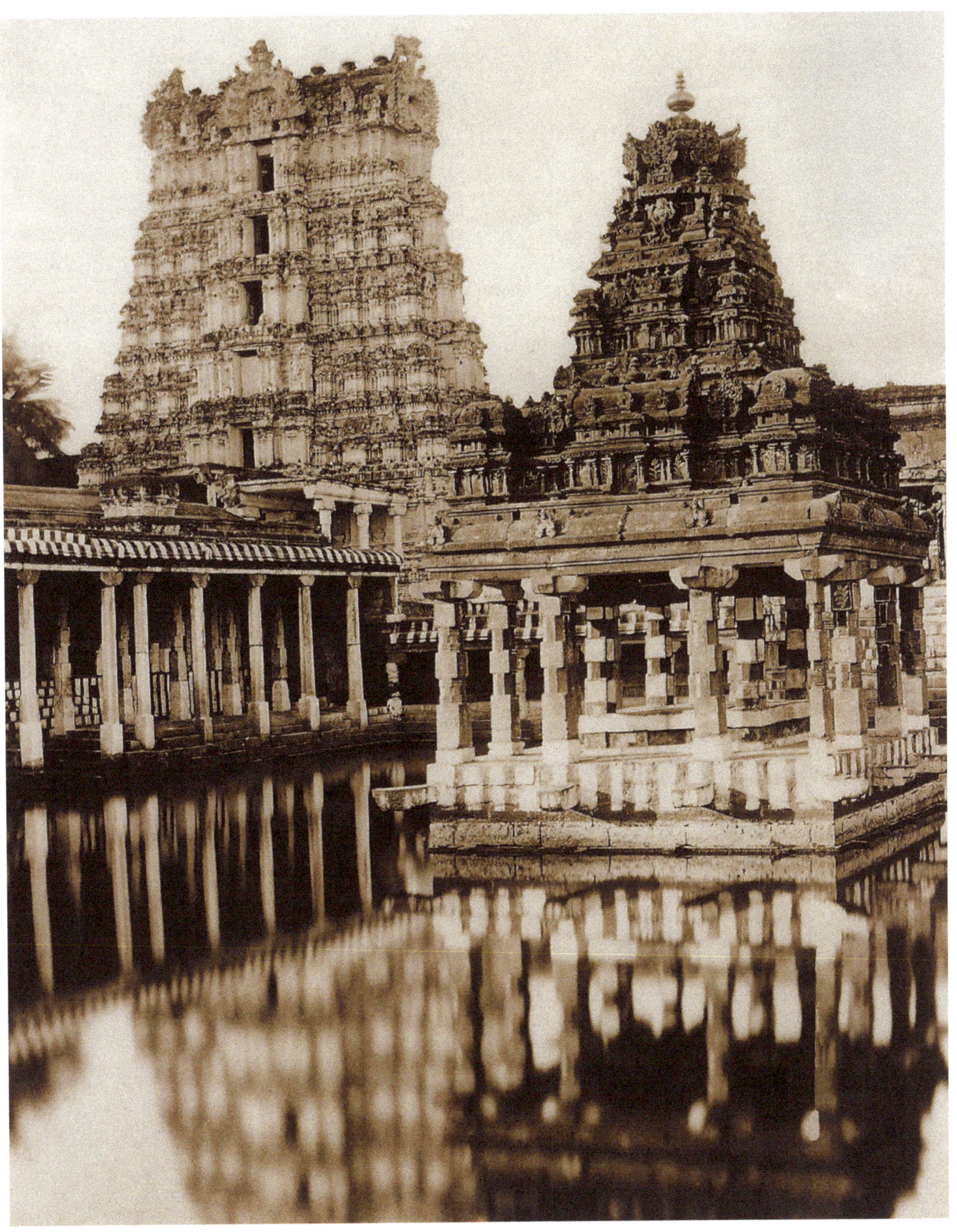

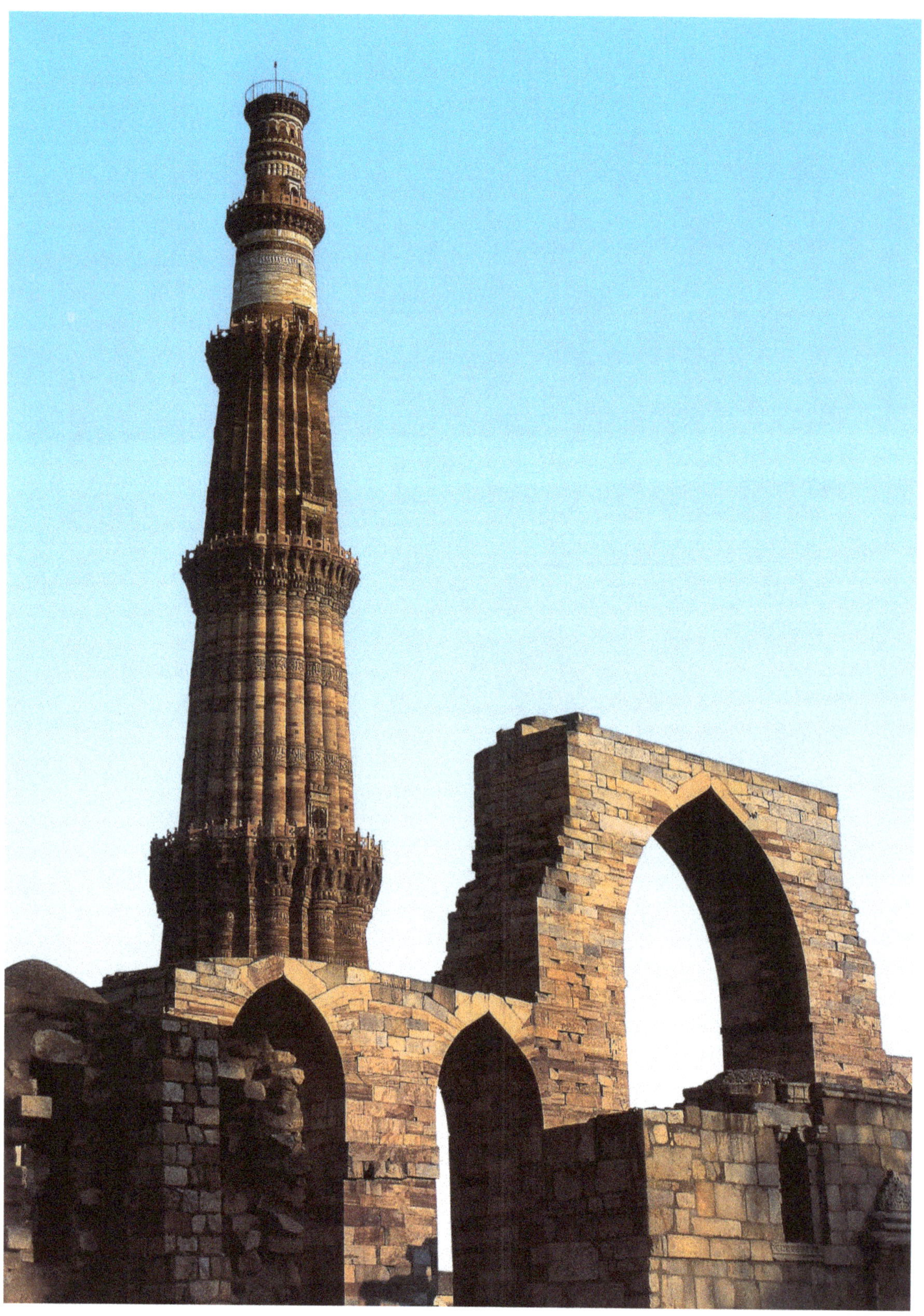

THE ISLAMIC PERIOD

The Indo-Islamic Styles of Architecture

The Islamic conquest in 712 C.E. of Sindh, (now part of Pakistan), did not seriously affect India proper, and the occupation of Kabul in 870 C.E. was equally without appreciable influence on Hindu polity, which continued its isolated course unchanged by external forces, developing on the political side the Rajput kingdoms, and on the aesthetic side the Brahmanical art already described. India did not feel the impact of Muslim ideas until the beginning of the eleventh century, when the repeated fierce raids of Mahmud of Ghazni compelled her to take notice of the new force. Before his death in 1030 C.E. the Punjab had become a province of the Islamic Sultanate of Ghazni. But, until the closing years of the twelfth century, Islam made no further progress in India. The early Arab conquerors of Sind seem to have left nothing but ruined Hindu temples behind them.

◀ *Qutb Minar*, 1192-1368, Sultanate period (Delhi). Red and buff sandstone, tower: diameter at the base: 14.32 m, at the top 2.75 m, height: 72.5 m. Mehrauli, Delhi.

The history of Indo-Islamic art begins with the year 1200 C.E. Between 1193 and 1236 C.E. Muhammad of Ghor, Qutb-ud-din Aibak, and Sultan Altamsh had compelled all northern India, including Bengal, to submit to the Muslim government established at Delhi. The earliest Islamic monuments in India date from the reigns of the three princes named; the principal works of that time being the mosque at Ajmer, the Qutb mosque and minor at Delhi, the gateway of the chief mosque at Budaun (1223 C.E.), and the tomb of the Sultan Altamsh at Delhi.

At the Qutb mosque of Delhi the glory of the building is the screen of eleven pointed arches, eight smaller and three larger, Muslim in form, but Hindu in construction. The faces of these structures are decorated with a lacework of intricate and delicate carving. It bears some resemblance to the decorations of certain parts of Santa Sophia at Constantinople.

Muslim usage requires that the faithful should be summoned to prayer at the stated times by a loud call uttered by a *muazzin*. In order to facilitate his duty many mosques, were furnished with one or two minarets. The Qutb Minar at Delhi is the most remarkable example of the detached minaret in existence. Like the adjoining mosque, it derives its familiar name from the saint.

The magnificent gateway erected in 1310 C.E. by the Sultan Alauddin Khilji on the south side of the enlarged Qutb Mosque marks an advance in Indo-Islamic architecture. Here the true arches with keystones were no longer constrained to execute the designs of their foreign masters by the structurally inferior Hindu methods.

The Kings or Sultans of the Tughlak dynasty of Delhi in the fourteenth century introduced a new style of architecture marked by massiveness and extreme simplicity. The most characteristic example of this severe style is the tomb of Ghiyath al-din Tughlak, who was killed by a carefully devised 'accident' in 1324. The style is more or less unique.

Under the patronage of its independent kings, Bengal developed an Islamic style of its own. An important characteristic of the style is the curvilinear cornice copied from bamboo structures. The buildings at Mandu, the capital of the kingdom of Malwa, which was independent from 1401 to 1531, are purely Muslim in style, closely related to those of the Sultans of Delhi.

Unquestionably, the most beautiful of the provincial styles of Muslim architecture in Northern and Western India is that of Gujarat. By good fortune it has been studied more carefully than any other Indian style. The style is that of the late medieval Hindu and Jain temples with such modifications as were necessary for the purposes of Muslim worship, and are characterized by all the richness of ornament distinctive of the temples of Gujarat and southern Rajasthan.

By far the most important of the Deccan styles is that of Bijapur. The buildings in it date between the years 1557 and 1686. The most ornate is the comparatively small tomb of Ibrahim Adil Shah II (1579-1626). The stately tomb of Muhammad Adil Shah (1636-1660) is covered with a dome the second largest in the world, a wonder of constructive skill, balanced internally by an ingenious arrangement of pendentives. The external ordonnance of this building is as beautiful as that of the interior. At each angle stands an octagonal tower eight storeys high, simple and bold in its proportions, and crowned by a dome of great elegance, relieved by two minarets.

Babur, the versatile founder of the Mughal dynasty, was an active builder during his brief and stormy Indian reign of five years (1526-1531). Out of the numerous edifices erected to Babur's order at Agra, Delhi, Kabul, and other places, only two are now visible, namely, the large mosque in the Kabul Bagh, Panipat, built after the great victory of 1526, and the Jami Masjid at Sambhal in Uttar Pradesh, bearing the same date.

The splendid mausoleum of Humayun, near Delhi, erected early in Akbar's reign, while distinctly Persian in style, is differentiated by the free use of white marble, a material little employed in Persia, and by the abstinence from colored tile decoration

▶ The Alai Darwaza (Alai Gate) is the main gateway of the southern side of the Quwwat-ul-Islam Mosque. Next to it is Imam Zamin's Tomb, 1311, Sultanate period (Delhi). Façade: red sandstone, inlay: white marble. Mehrauli, Delhi.

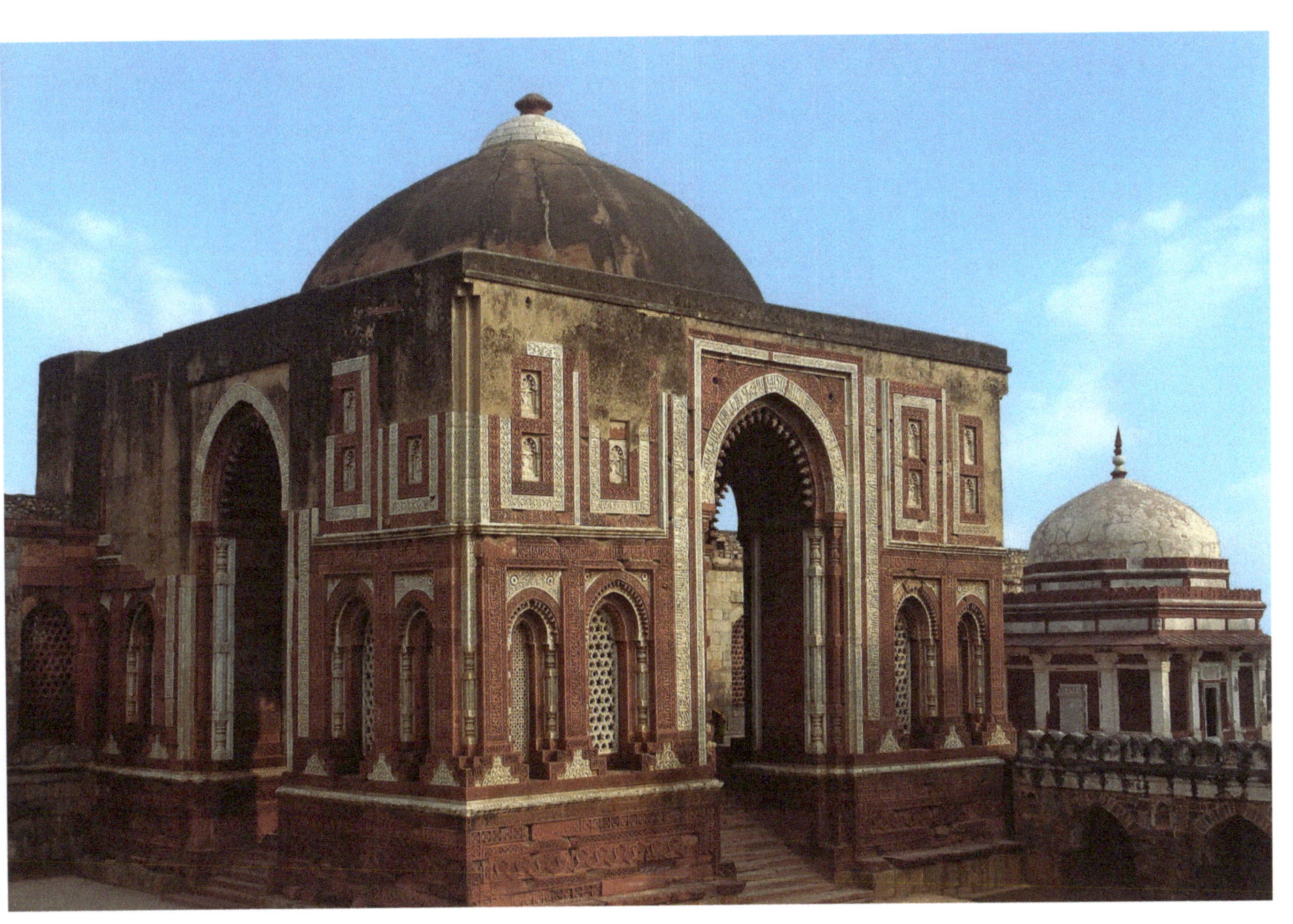

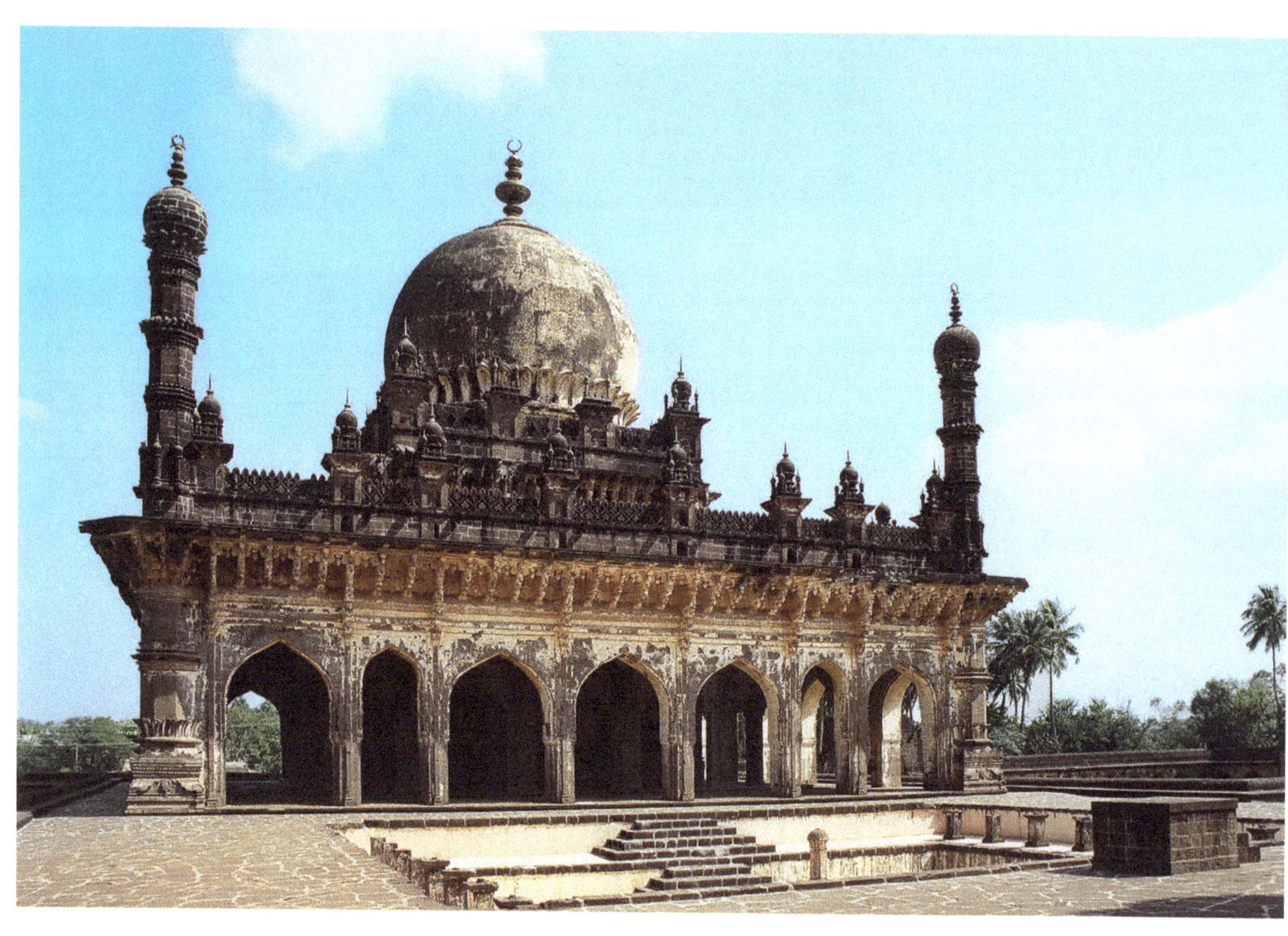

so much favored by the architects of that country. The building is of special interest as being to some extent the model of the inimitable 'Taj'. The dome is built entirely of white marble, the rest of the masonry being in red sandstone, with inlaid ornaments of white marble.

The magnificent mausoleum of Akbar at Sikandra near Agra is exceptional. It is composed of five square terraces, diminishing as they ascend. In all oriental houses and palaces the roof plays a part of great importance in daily life. From the earliest times, it was used as an additional room, being covered by awnings and screened in. These hangings, which were beautifully dyed and embroidered, are indispensable in Mughal architectural planning, being hung from pillar to pillar or supported on finely worked staffs.

Passing by other notable buildings of Jahangir's reign at Lahore (now a part of Pakistan) and elsewhere, we come to the reign of his son Shah Jahan (1627-1658), during which the Indo-Persian style, by universal consent, attained supreme beauty in the Taj Mahal (1632-1653), the Moti Masjid, or Pearl Mosque at Agra (1646-1653), and the palace at Delhi, begun in 1638.

The style is essentially Persian, but with an indefinable difference of expression, and sharply

◀ *Ibrahim Rouza (Tomb of Ibrahim Adil Shah II, 1556-1627),* 1626, Deccani sultanates period, Adil Shahi dynasty. Rock. Bijapur, Karnataka.

distinguished from the fashions of Isfahan as well as those of Constantinople by the lavish use of white marble, carved and fretted, and supplemented by sumptuous decoration in pietra dura inlay and other enrichments. Openwork tracery of incomparable beauty is a marked feature, and spacious grandeur of design is successfully combined with feminine elegance. It is impossible to exaggerate descriptions of the magnificence of the Delhi palace, nor is there any need to insist on the unearthly loveliness of the Taj, one of the noblest monuments ever erected to man or woman.

The immense enclosed complex of buildings and gardens familiarly designated as 'the Taj', comprises the central mausoleum, the mosque on the west, a corresponding edifice (*jawab*) on the east, intended as a place of assembly buildings for the congregation of the mosque and the persons invited to the annual commemoration services; huge gateways with many chambers, massive enclosing walls, and various minor structures, some of which have been ruined.

The purpose of all was to honor the memory of Shah Jahan's well-beloved wife, the Empress Arjumand Banu Begum, whose title Mumtaz Mahal ('The Chosen One of the Palace') has been corrupted into Taj. The villas and tombs of the great nobles and many other buildings, few of which remain, once crowded the approaches and surrounding space.

The wondrous tomb destined to give her immortal fame was begun early in 1632 C.E., corresponding to the fifth year of Shah Jahan's reign. When the plans had been settled to the Emperor's satisfaction

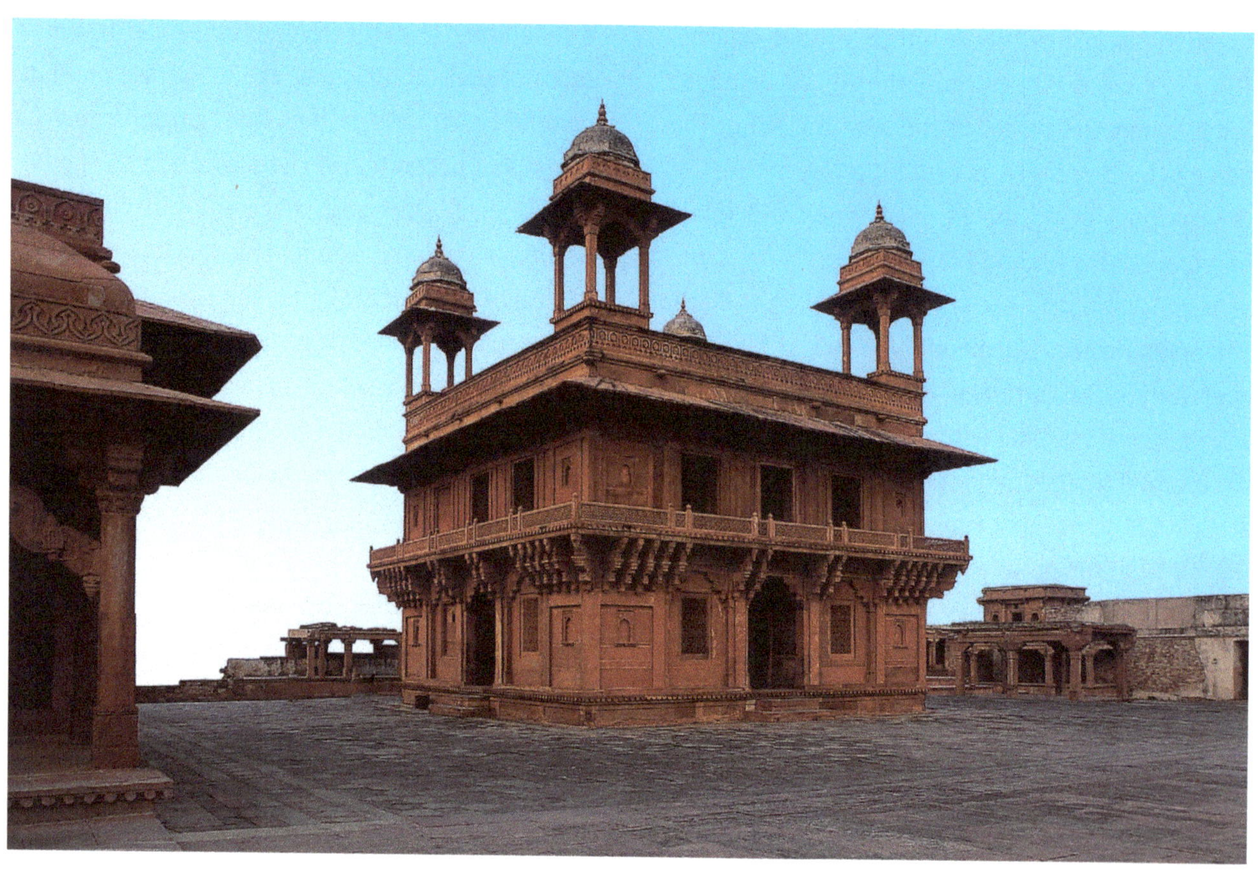

▲ *Diwan-i-Khas (Hall of Private Audience)*, c. 1571,
Mughal dynasty (Akbar). Red sandstone.
Fatehpur Sikri, Uttar Pradesh.

work was pushed on with eagerness, some 20,000 men being employed daily. On 6 February 1643, the annual funeral ceremony was celebrated by the bereaved husband at the new mausoleum which was then regarded as complete.

Shah Jahan planned for himself a mausoleum of equal magnificence to be erected on the opposite side of the river and united with the Taj by a marble bridge, but his family troubles prevented the realization of this gigantic conception, and so he sleeps beside the 'Lady of the Taj'. 'They were lovely and pleasant in their lives and in their death they were not divided.'

The long and unhappy reign of Aurangzeb Alamgir (1659-1707) was marked by a rapid decline in art, including architecture. The emperor was more eager to throw down Hindu temples than to construct great edifices. Some few buildings of his time, however, are not without merit; for instance, the tall minarets of the mosque which he caused to be erected at Varanasi on the site of the holiest temple are well known to all travelers in India.

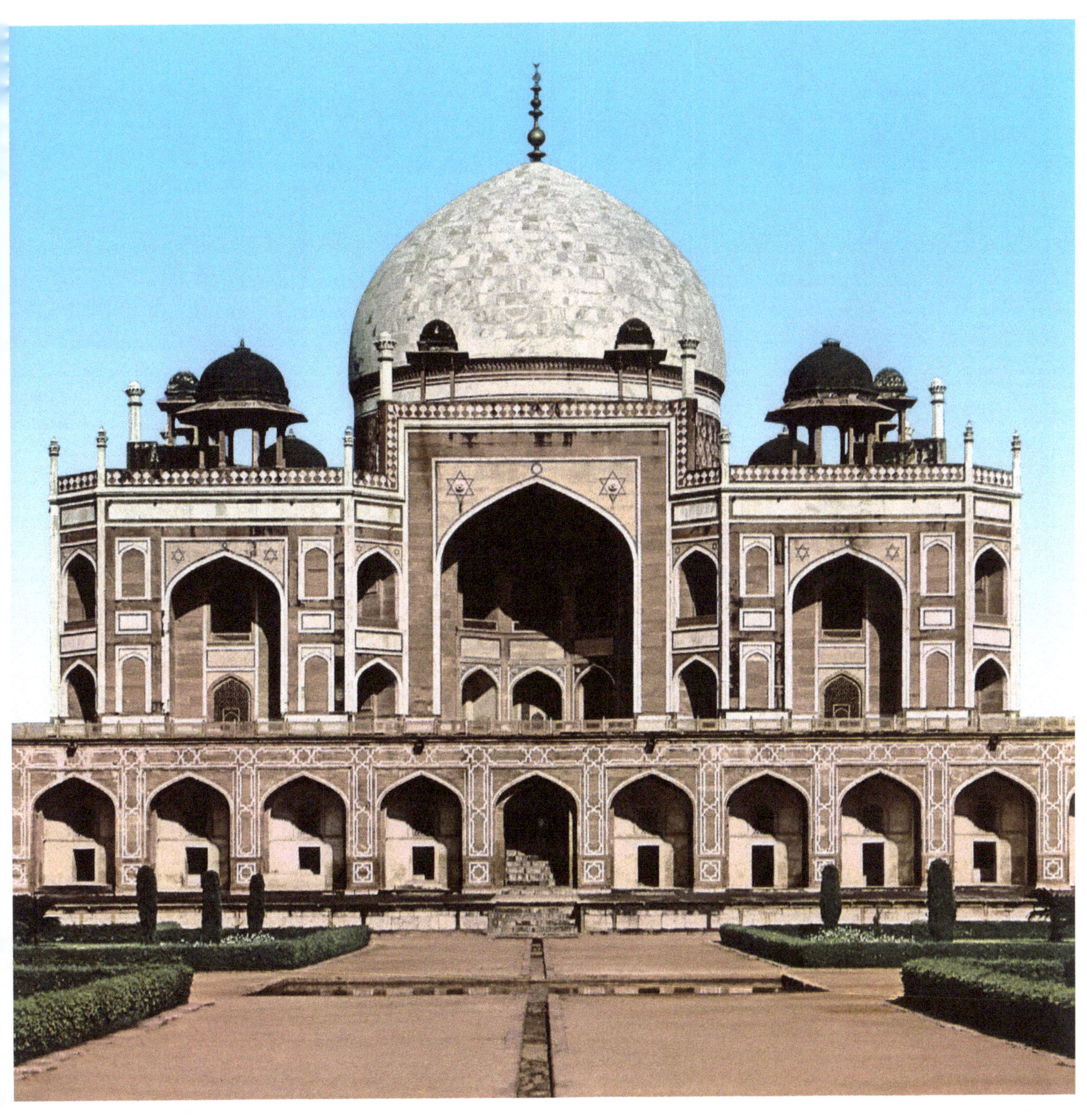

▲ *Humayun Mausoleum*, 1556,
Mughal dynasty (Humayun).
Red sandstone. Delhi.

▼ *Badshahi Mosque*, 1671-1673, Mughal dynasty
(Aurangzeb). Façade: red sandstone, inlay:
white marble. Lahore, Punjab.

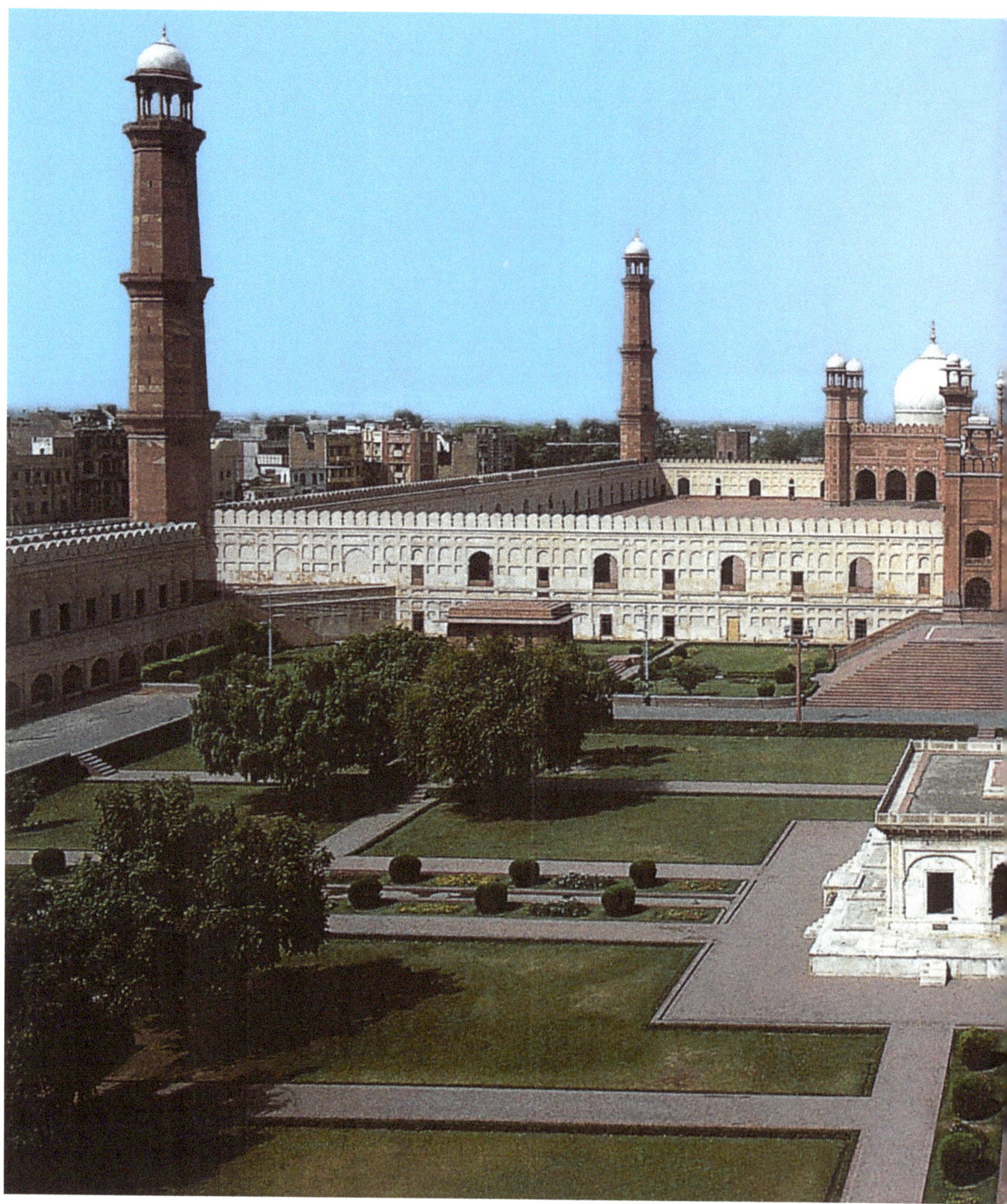

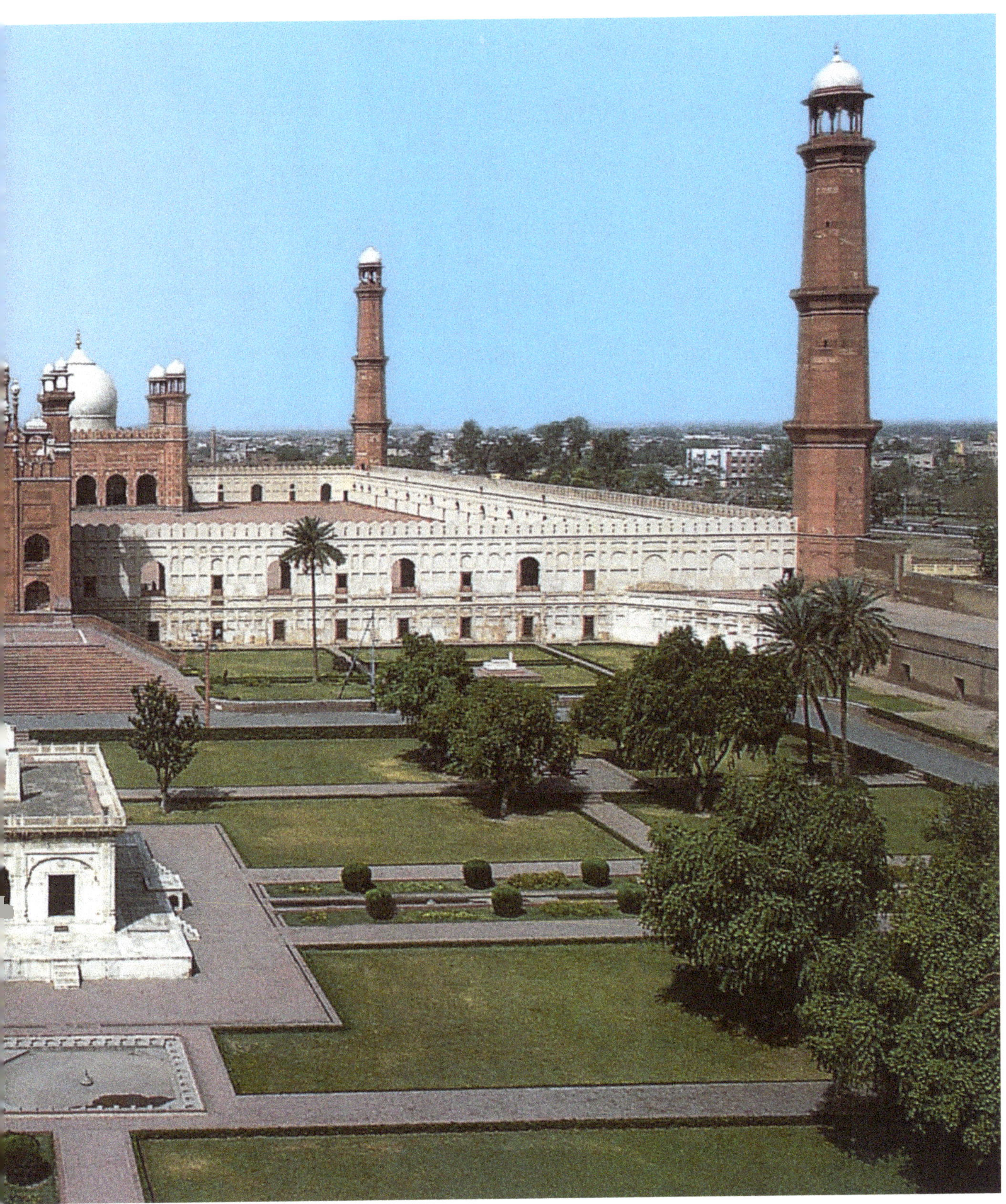

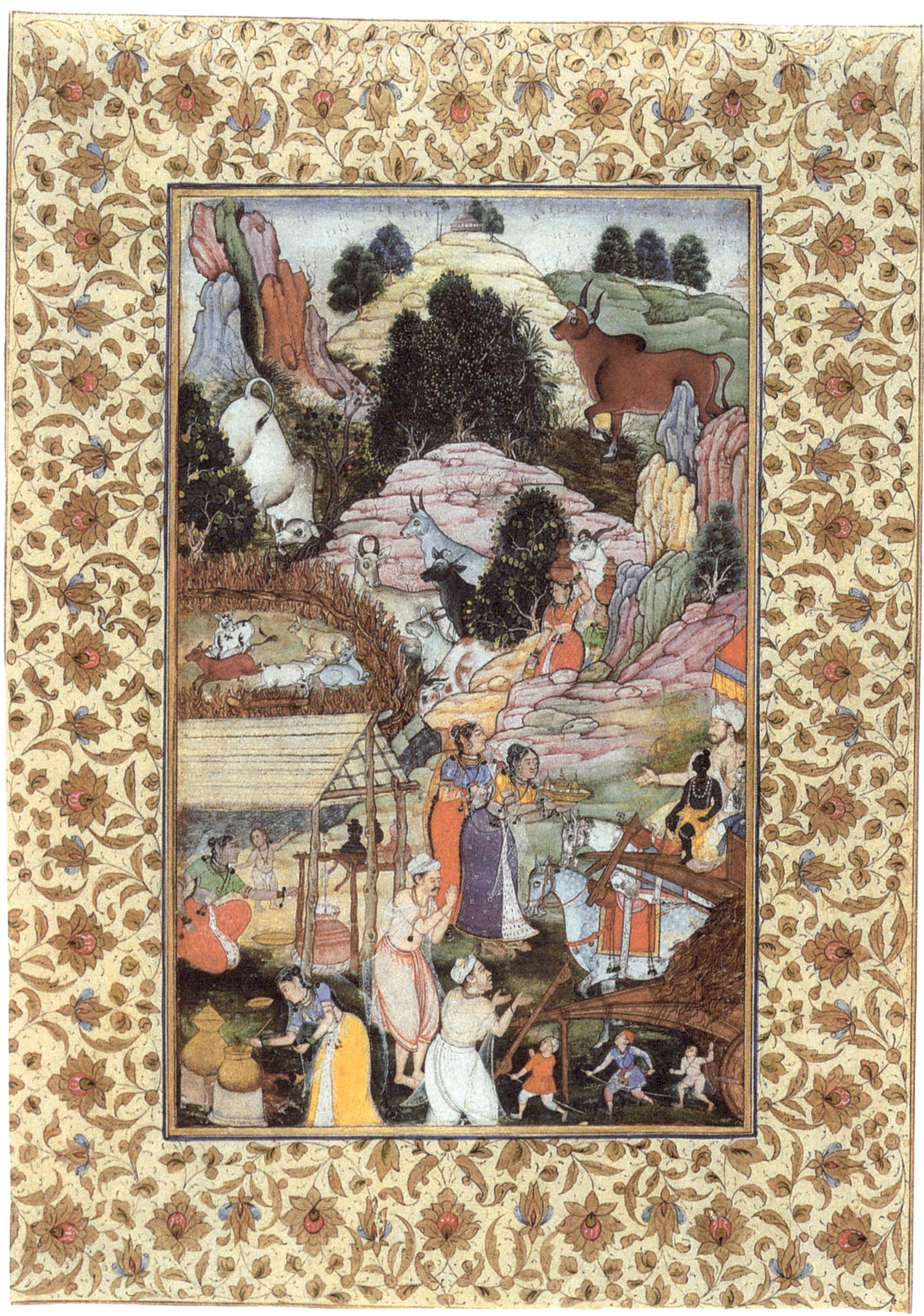

THE INDO-ISLAMIC STYLES OF PAINTING

Gujarati Painting

Indian miniature painting is divided into two, the foreign Islamic school which rose under Persian tuition during the reigns of the Mughal emperors, and in contradistinction, an ancient, indigenous, wholly Indian school, which is designated 'Rajput', persisting 'in Rajasthan and the Himalayas up to the end of the eighteenth century, comparatively little affected by the Persian and European influences which enter so largely into the art of the Mughal Court. Rajput painting is related to the classic art of Ajanta, as the Hindu language and literature are related to the older Prakrits and to Sanskrit. The Rajput paintings, indeed, show a remarkable combination of folk idioms with ancient hieratic design.' Mughal art, on the other hand, is a purely miniature art, unrelated to the ancient Indian frescoes. It is courtly not popular, secular not religious, material not spiritual.

◄ *Page from a Manuscript of the Harivamsha: The Arrival of Nanda and His Family in Vrindavan*, 1586-1590, Mughal dynasty (Akbar), Gujarat, Patan. Opaque watercolour and ink on paper, 40.8 x 30 cm.
Virginia Museum of Fine Arts, Richmond, Virginia

Mughal Painting

The history of Mughal painting begins with the name of Mir Sayyid Ali. In the year 1525 Babur set out upon the conquest of India, a land, however, of which he did not conceive highly. Five years later he was dead. In 1546 Humayun, his son, was deprived of his empire by the Afghan, Sher Shah, and until his final victory in 1555 existed as a landless refugee. One year of this period was spent at the Safavid court at Tabriz, where Shah Tahmasp now ruled. Another painter of growing reputation attracted the notice of the exiled emperor; this was Abdul Samad.

In 1550 both these artists joined Humayun's court at Kabul. It was here that Mir Sayyid Ali was commissioned to supervise the illustration of the romance of Amir Hamzah in twelve volumes of a hundred folios each. Sixty of these illustrations painted in tempera colors on prepared cotton cloth are in Vienna, and twenty-five of them in the Indian Gallery of the Victoria and Albert Museum and the British Museum. They must probably be attributed to the artists of the imperial court working under Mir Sayyid Ali, rather than to that painter himself.

Akbar succeeded to the insecure throne of his father when still a boy. The culture of his court did not merely reflect at a distance the splendor of Bukhara and Samarkand. The building of Fatehpur Sikri in 1569 heralded a new era of Indian rule. And after the architects, masons, and sculptors had done their work, painters were called in to decorate the walls of the public halls and private apartments. The rapidity with which the teaching of Abdul Samad and his Islamic colleagues was assimilated and then modified by scores of Hindu artists of various castes is in itself sufficient proof that the foreign teachers must have found trained indigenous scholars with whom to work. Men accustomed to draw and paint could easily learn new methods and a foreign style, but not even the despotic power of Akbar would have been able to create a numerous school of Hindu artists out of nothing.

The Koran, following the Semitic principle formulated in the Mosaic The second Commandment, absolutely forbids Muslims to make likenesses of anything in heaven or on earth; and the prohibition has been and is strictly obeyed, with rare exceptions, in all countries and at all times, so far as the decoration of mosques and other buildings devoted to religious purposes is concerned. In book illustrations, however, such liberty is commonly assumed. The Mughal emperors of India looked to Iran for the graces of civilization, and it was natural that Akbar should desire to add the charms of Persian pictorial art to the amenities of his court. Regarding himself as Head of the Church and pontiff of a new religion, he cared little about the Prophet.

He found no difficulty in gratifying his taste. Liberal pay and abundant honor drew crowds of artists, foreigners and Indians, Muslims and Hindus, to his magnificent court, where the more distinguished were enrolled as *mansabdars*, or members of the official nobility, and assigned ample salaries.

Excepting the modern Delhi miniatures on ivory, the frescoes, the early paintings on cotton, and a few pictures on vellum, the Indo-Persian paintings are all executed on paper. No Indian examples of painting on silk in the Chinese manner are known. The Indo-Persian, like other Asiatic artists, conceived every object as being bounded by firm lines, and consequently, his first step was the drawing of an outline. For the illustration of ordinary Persian books, the outline drawn directly on the page in red or black chalk was filled in with colors at once. Jewels and ornaments were indicated by needle prickings in sheets of gold leaf, or even by the insertion of pearls or diamond chips. The work was all done by the Indian artists with fine squirrel-hair brushes, the most delicate strokes being executed with a brush of a single hair, an instrument requiring the utmost correctness of eye and steadiness of hand.

The practice of beginning a picture by laying down a firmly drawn outline led to a curious division of labor, the outline often being drawn by one man and the painting done by another. Sometimes four

Attributed to an artist of Golconde, Azam Shah (1653-1707).
From the illuminated manuscript the History of India from Tamerlane (1336-1405) to Aurangzeb (1618-1707), 1678-1686, Mughal dynasty (Aurangzeb). Gouache, gold and silver, 31.5 x 22 cm; paper folio 37 x 26.5 cm. Bibliothèque nationale de France, Paris.

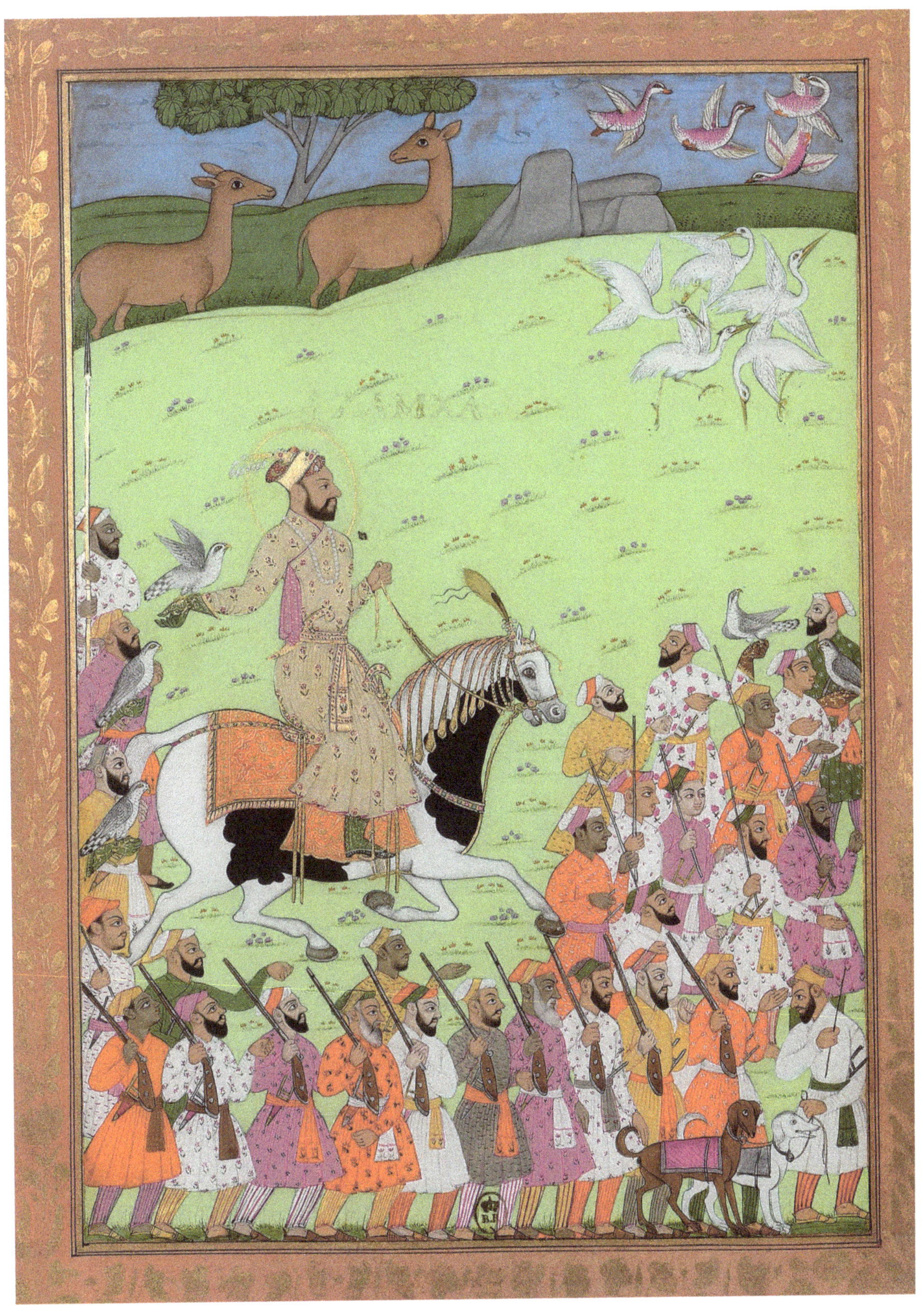

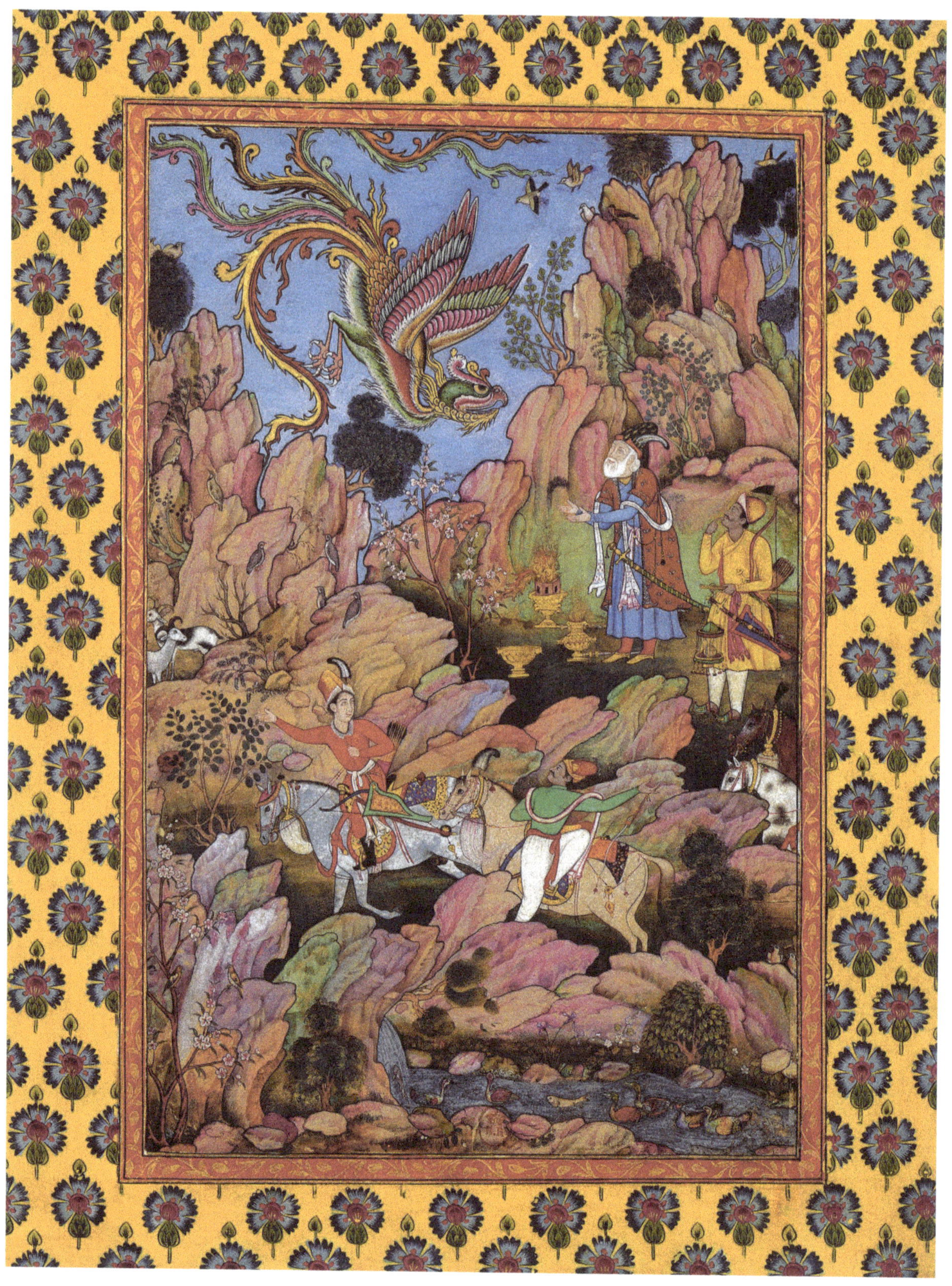

artists collaborated in one work. It is not clear how such a complicated arrangement was worked. The method necessarily tended to reduce their art to the level of a skilled mechanical craft. The early Indo-Persian book illustrations are wrought in excessively brilliant colors, chiefly red, yellow, and blue.

During Akbar's reign (1556-1605) and a portion of Jahangir's (1605-1627) the standing portrait figures are usually represented in profile in a formal, conventional manner, with the right hand holding up a flower or jewel, and the feet placed one in front of the other. Gradually this stiff formalism was dropped, and men and women were drawn in natural attitudes. The more ancient Indo-Persian works, like their Persian models, follow unreservedly a style marked by the total lack of roundness, depth of tone, and aerial perspective, every object being represented as absolutely flat. During the later years of Jahangir's reign and subsequently, this flat style was modified by the Indian artists, who frequently introduced slight line shading with admirable effect, so contriving to give their figures a sufficient degree of roundness with wonderfully few strokes.

The Indo-Persian or Mughal school of drawing and painting having lived in considerable vigor from about 1570 to 1830 a period, roughly speaking, of two centuries and a half and not being quite dead until the twentieth century, naturally produced an enormous output. The extant works, notwithstanding all the mishaps to which Indian art has been exposed, still can be numbered by thousands. Although the long-continued political and social agony which accompanied the decline and fall of the Mughal empire necessarily limited the opportunities for the practice of art, art did not die; a synthesis between Hindu tradition and Persian technique produced a new variety of Indian pictorial art possessing high merits.

The Indo-Persian artists excelled in the delineation of animals, both quadrupeds and birds. The celebrated artist Ustad Mansur, who enjoyed the special favor of Jahangir, and was honored by him with a title of nobility, began his career in Akbar's reign. The Waqiat-i-Baburi contains a series of eight exquisite little miniatures from his brush. Mansur excelled as an animal and bird painter.

Indo-Persian art attained its highest achievements during the reign of the magnificent Shah Jahan (1627-1658 C.E.), when the land enjoyed comparative peace, and a luxurious court offered liberal encouragement to all artists capable of ministering to its pleasure. The fierce scenes of bloodshed in which the earlier artists delighted were replaced by pageants of peaceful courtly splendor, the old aggressive coloring was toned down or dispensed with, and a general refinement of style and execution was cultivated. Perfectly drawn elephants are numerous. Indian artists, whether sculptors or painters, rarely failed to produce good representations of the huge quadruped.

A favorite subject was the story of Baz Bahadur, king of Malwa, and his lady-love, Princess Rupmati, who are represented in several pictures as riding together by torchlight. Other romances frequently illustrated are the tales of Laila and Majnun, Khusrau and Shirin, and Kamrup and Kamta.

Several pictures are extant which exhibit this contrast in scenes of hunting by night, flaming torches being used to dazzle and hypnotize the deer. The same motive, which also attracted Rembrandt, inspires the pictures representing a lady standing on a balcony watching the effect of fireworks over the dark waters of the Jumna.

During the reigns of Aurangzeb (1658-1707) and his decadent successors, we find the artists still numerous and specimens of their work are abundant. Although Aurangzeb was too zealous a puritan to care for art himself, the fashion set by his predecessors had not died out, and princes and nobles still kept court painters. Portraiture continued to be practiced with great success, although the execution rarely attains the perfection of the first half of the seventeenth century. The art of this period and subsequent periods can only be justly treated of as the product of artists who gained a living at minor courts, Hindu or Muslim, and whose style and choice of subjects are modified by the local demand.

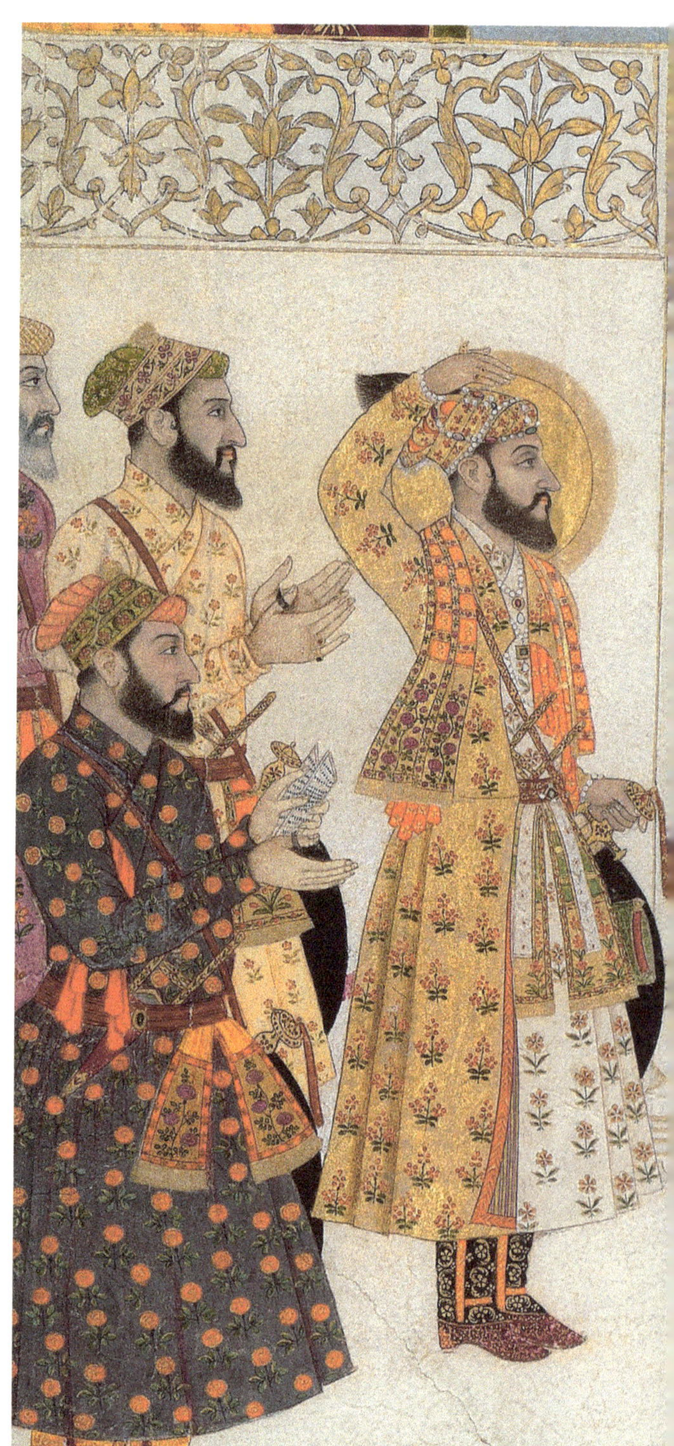

▶ *Durbar (audience) of Shah Jahan (1592-1666) in Lahore (present-day Pakistan) where he receives Aurangzeb (1618-1707) (detail)*, c. 1670, Mughal dynasty (Aurangzeb). Gouache and gold, 31.2 x 23.4 cm; folio 42 x 25 cm. Bibliothèque nationale de France, Paris.

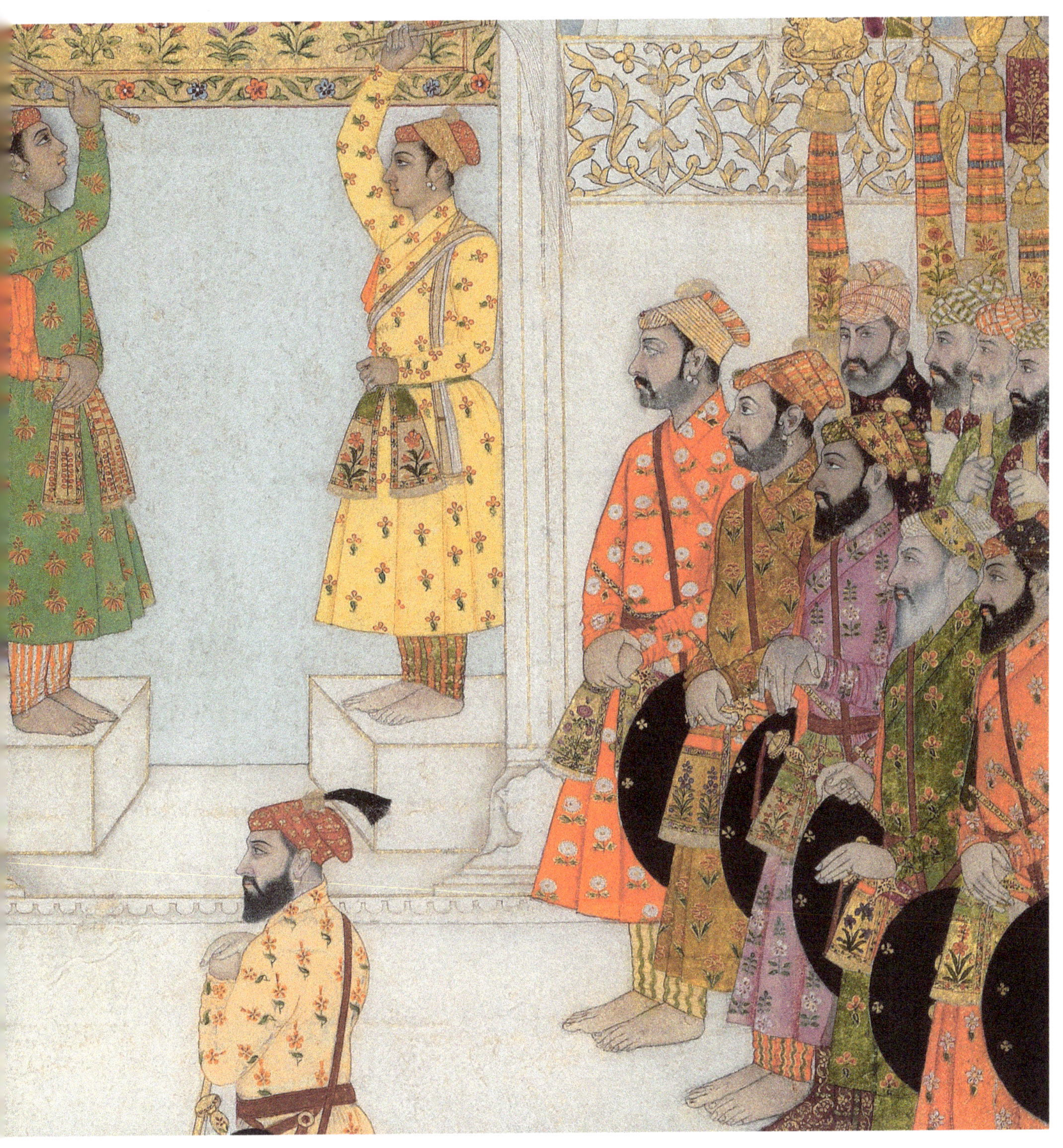

LIST OF ILLUSTRATIONS

ART HISTORY COLLECTION

- Abstract Art
- Art Deco
- Art Nouveau
- Baroque
- Byzantine Art
- Chinese Art
- Cubism
- Dada
- Early Italian Art
- Egypt Art
- Expressionism
- Gothic Art
- Greek Art
- Impressionism
- Indian Art

- Naive Art
- Neoclassicism
- Persian Art
- Post-Impressionism
- Realism
- Renaissance
- Pre-Raphaelites
- Rococo
- Roman Art
- Romanesque Art
- Romanticism
- Surrealism
- Symbolism
- The Fauves
- The Viennese Secession